United States
Department
of Agriculture

Forest Service

**Rocky Mountain
Research Station**

General Technical
Report RMRS-GTR-284

August 2012

Vulnerability of Species to Climate Change in the Southwest: Threatened, Endangered, and At-Risk Species at the Barry M. Goldwater Range, Arizona

Karen E. Bagne and Deborah M. Finch

I0434781

ABSTRACT

Future climate change is anticipated to result in ecosystem changes, and consequently, many species are expected to become increasingly vulnerable to extinction. This scenario is of particular concern for threatened, endangered, and at-risk species (TER-S) or other rare species. The response of species to climate change is uncertain and will be the outcome of complex interactions and processes. Nevertheless, a simple flexible strategy is needed to help integrate climate change into management planning and actions. This assessment uses SAVS, an assessment tool based on ecological principals, to rank individual species of interest within the eastern portion of the Barry M. Goldwater Range, Arizona, according to predicted climate change responses and associated population declines balanced with responses expected to incur resilience or population increases. Further, specific areas of vulnerability, research needs, and management implications are identified for each species in detailed species accounts. Based solely on predicted response to climate change, Sonoran pronghorn (*Antilocapra americana sonoriensis*) and desert tortoise (*Gopherus morafkai*) are the most vulnerable to population declines. Results also suggest that climate change will make management of some TER-S species more difficult. Several critical management areas are identified that can mitigate negative impacts to benefit multiple species, including fire and fuels, invasive species, natural and artificial waters, and landscape-scale planning. Management planning should be in place that will assist species impacted by extreme events such as prolonged drought, severe wildfires, and/or intense flooding. The assessment process was also used to identify areas where climate change may present opportunities, as opposed to challenges, for species management.

Keywords: climate change, vulnerability, Southwest, Arizona, endangered species, SAVS

AUTHORS

Karen E. Bagne is a Wildlife Ecologist with the USDA Forest Service, Rocky Mountain Research Station.

Deborah M. Finch is the Program Manager for the Grassland, Shrubland, and Desert Ecosystem program of the USDA Forest Service, Rocky Mountain Research Station.

CONTENTS

Acknowledgments

This project was funded by the Department of Defense Legacy Resource Management Program (Project 09-433). Additional funding was provided by the USDA Forest Service. Information from the original report (posted on www.denix.osd.mil, August 2010) was updated to create this report.

We thank Richard Whittle and Daniel Garcia of Luke Air Force Base for their support. Megan Friggens produced Figure 3 and, along with Sharon Coe, provided review and discussion of climate change topics that improved this assessment. Collaborators that inspired assessment development include: Carolyn Enquist and David Gori of The Nature Conservancy, Lisa Graumlich at the University of Arizona, and Heather Bateman at Arizona State University Polytechnic. Further support and advice was provided by Jack Triepke and Bryce Rickel of USDA Forest Service, Rocky Mountain Region. Mary Bagne provided editing assistance.

Introduction

A large number of species are imperiled and at risk of extinction if populations continue to decline (Wilcove and Master 2005). Of Federal landholdings, those managed by the Department of Defense (DoD) harbor the most endangered or threatened species. Those lands also contain large numbers of species at risk—those that are imperiled but not yet listed as endangered or threatened by the U.S. Fish and Wildlife Service (USFWS) (NatureServe 2004). These species, also known as threatened, endangered, and at-risk species (TER-S) are an important element of natural resource management. For species that are not listed as Federally endangered or threatened, effective and proactive management of species at risk can prevent listing, reduce management costs, and protect biodiversity while insuring that critical military training is not disrupted (NatureServe 2004). Two endangered vertebrate species and several candidate species are known or have the potential to occur in the eastern portion of the Barry M. Goldwater Range (BMGR-East) in southern Arizona.

Over the past century, the climate in the southwestern United States has been becoming warmer and drier, and this trend is expected to continue (Field and others 2007). In fact, this region is projected to be subject to a significant change in climate that will have broad impacts on ecosystems. Because current climate conditions are already physiologically challenging, even small changes can exceed species' tolerances. There is a broad consensus among climate models that conditions will become more extreme (Archer and Predick 2008), which will have consequences for biodiversity. While the exact nature of these consequences is unknown, shifts in species distributions and changes in populations are highly likely. Declining populations and eventual extinction is of increasing concern for species already at high extinction risk that are expected to experience negative impacts from climate change.

Climate change is a new challenge for natural resource managers that has the potential to exacerbate existing management issues and create new ones. Preservation of biodiversity will be particularly challenging and few strategies have been proposed to guide managers (Lucier and others 2006). Species assessments of vulnerability or extinction risk are management tools used to help prioritize conservation needs so that actions can be directed in an effective and efficient manner (Glick and others 2011). Species can be ranked based on assessment outcome, but implementation of management actions will also be constrained by goals, economics, politics, and feasibility. To include climate change in a vulnerability assessment is a challenging task because the strongest climate change effects are not yet manifest, global carbon and nitrogen cycling are complex, species vary in sensitivity and adaptive capacity, and direct effects on relatively few species have been identified. To ignore climate change is to risk being unable to respond to a biodiversity crisis (McLaughlin and others 2002; Early and Sax 2011).

Climate Change Assessment

Purpose

Anticipation of future impacts of changing climate can help ameliorate those impacts through early intervention—a key factor for balancing ongoing and uninterrupted military operations with cost-effective natural resource management.

Resources for management are also limited, thus priority targets and actions need to be identified (see Box 1). The purpose of this assessment is to address the vulnerability of individual TER-S to population declines associated with projected changes in climate at BMGR-East in southern Arizona. Pertinent projections for climate and biotic communities, from which climate change response is predicted, are summarized from the current literature. Species are ranked by anticipated vulnerability, and potential management actions are suggested based on the specific vulnerabilities identified. The interaction of climate change variables with currently known threats to species is also discussed.

Box 1. Why assess vulnerability?

Vulnerability is the susceptibility to negative impact. Vulnerability assessments help us identify where negative impacts are likely to occur and why. In this assessment, we define the vulnerability of terrestrial vertebrate species to climate change as likely declines in populations through either reduced survival or reproduction. Managers that use vulnerability assessments can:

1. Help set priorities and prepare for the future
2. Identify adaptation strategies that target predicted effects
3. Make more efficient use of scarce resources

Modified from Glick and others (2011)

Approach

Vulnerability of species to climate change will depend on sensitivity, exposure, and adaptive capacity (Glick and others 2011). We used the System for Assessing Vulnerability of Species (SAVS) to rank vulnerability of terrestrial vertebrates to climate change (Bagne and others 2011). This tool scores individual species based on basic ecology and life history traits that are related to climate. Traits related to sensitivity and adaptive capacity are integrated into the system, and exposure, or future projection, is considered but taken from published sources prior to scoring. Scores are the balance of a set of 22 traits that predict vulnerability (i.e., reduced survival or reproduction), resilience (i.e., increased survival or reproduction), or no change. Because the same set of traits is applied to all species, scores can be used to compare vulnerability of a set of species. The system produces an overall score and four category scores for habitat, physiology, phenology, and interactions as well as uncertainty for these scores. Each score is the balance of the number of vulnerable versus resilient traits, with all traits weighted equally and adjusted to a common scale (see Bagne and others 2011 for details). Uncertainty is based on the availability of information or in cases of opposing predictions for an individual question. We used a spreadsheet to aid score calculations, but calculations can also be made by hand following Bagne and others (2011) or on the SAVS web site (http://www.fs.fed.us/rmrs/species-vulnerability/). Traits associated with vulnerability for an individual species or that are common across several species are used to identify management actions to reduce vulnerability.

We developed and used a similar but separate pilot scoring tool to predict individual plant species' vulnerability. The plant species vulnerability pilot tool is available at: http://denix.osd.mil/nr/OtherConservationTopicsAH/ClimateChange. cfm. That tool produces an overall score and three category scores for habitat, physiology, and interactions as well as uncertainty for these scores in the same manner as SAVS.

Scope

Predicted species response and vulnerability scores are based on available projections of how climate and related phenomena are expected to change in the region of interest. Unlike the vertebrate species tool, the plant vulnerability tool is integrated with specific climate projections and is, thus, restricted to the southwestern United States. For this assessment, we focused on projections up to the next 50 years. The specific projections used for the assessment follow this section.

We assessed species with known or suspected occurrence in BMGR-East listed by USFWS as endangered or threatened (Figure 1). We also included additional species that are either proposed or under review for Federal listing or of high conservation priority for Arizona as identified by the State Wildlife Action Plan (AGFD 2006). To provide information on a more diverse array of taxa, we also scored some species that were not identified as at risk, but were identified as conservation elements in the proposed biodiversity management framework (Hall and others 2001). We limited this report to terrestrial vertebrate and vascular plant species. No plants were identified from the eastern portion of the range that were Federally endangered or threatened. We assessed one plant species that potentially occurs on BMGR-East, the acuña cactus, which is a candidate for listing. Prioritization and identification of vulnerabilities are presented separately for vertebrates and plants.

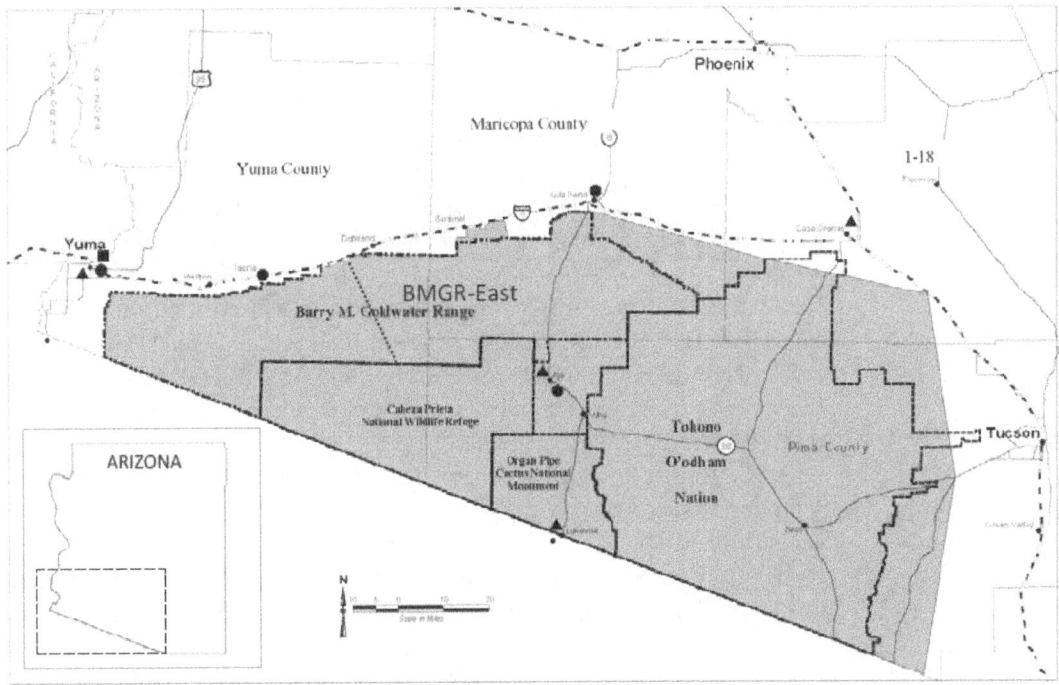

Figure 1. Map of Barry M. Goldwater Range and vicinity showing BMGR-East assessed in this document. Map modified from INRMP (2003).

Projections of Climate, Disturbance, and Biotic Communities

Current and Future Climate

The Southwest is characterized by a hot and arid climate, which is also highly variable because of its geographical location and positioning between two circulation regimes (Sheppard and others 2002). BMGR-East lies in a particularly hot and arid part of the region, but with considerable variability from east to west and from high to low elevations. High summer temperatures at nearby Gila Bend, averaged over the period 1892 to 2000, were over 38 °C (100 °F) with a maximum of 50 °C (122 °F) (INMRP 2003). In winter, average temperatures range from 4 °C to 24 °C (40 °F to 75 °F). Recorded temperatures already indicate that the region is warming at a rate unprecedented in the last 400 years (Sheppard and others 2002). There is also evidence of fewer days below freezing and an increase in winter temperatures for the Sonoran Desert (Weiss and Overpeck 2005). With increasing levels of carbon dioxide (CO_2), average annual temperature is expected to increase approximately 2.2 °C (4 °F) by 2050 (www.climatewizard.org, PRISM group, United States mid-century, 12-km resolution, downscaling based on Maurer and others 2007). These estimates may be too low as recent emission rates have exceeded those used to forecast future climate (from preliminary 2009 and 2010 global and national estimates of carbon emissions, http://cdiac.ornl.gov).

Precipitation in the region falls in winter and in summer with a dry period from April to June (INRMP 2003). Average annual precipitation declines from east to west with 21.7 cm (8.5 inches) per year in Ajo, on the southeastern edge of BMGR-East, and 11 cm (4.33 inches) per year at Tacna, near the northwestern edge. Rainfall is higher in the mountains and may be up to 28 cm (11 inches) per year (INRMP 2003). Shifting of circulation patterns associated with the El Niño Southern Oscillation (ENSO) and the Pacific Decadal Oscillation (PDO) alters winter precipitation patterns in the Southwest. Winters are wetter during El Niño when the westerly flow of moist air across North America shifts southward and are drier during La Niña when the flow shifts to the north. Changes in PDO enhance or dampen ENSO patterns (Shepperd and others 2002). During the summer, westerly winds diminish and a high pressure ridge forms signaling the start of the monsoon season, which brings moisture to the region from the Gulf of Mexico and the Gulf of California (Shepperd and others 2002). Unlike the widespread gentle rains of winter, the monsoons bring intense thunderstorms with highly variable local rainfall, which affects water uptake by soil and vegetation. Summer monsoonal rains fall principally in July and August and primarily on the eastern parts of BMGR-East. Monsoon patterns in this subregion differ from monsoons to the east in New Mexico, which come earlier and last into September, and monsoons to the south in Mexico, which also last longer and have much higher precipitation totals (Figure 2; Comrie and Glenn 1998).

Projections for precipitation are more varied than those for temperature. In one set of models, projections for winter rain (December to February) are approximately unchanged for 2050 under the current emissions rate and averaged circulation models (www.climatewizard.org, PRISM group, United States mid-century, 12-km resolution, downscaling based on Maurer and others 2007). Other studies predict drying of the Southwest driven by changes in humidity and atmospheric circulation (Seager and others 2007). Periodic La Niña conditions in conjunction with a drying of the region are projected to bring severe and prolonged droughts (Seager and others 2007; Cook and others 2009). Predictions for summer monsoon

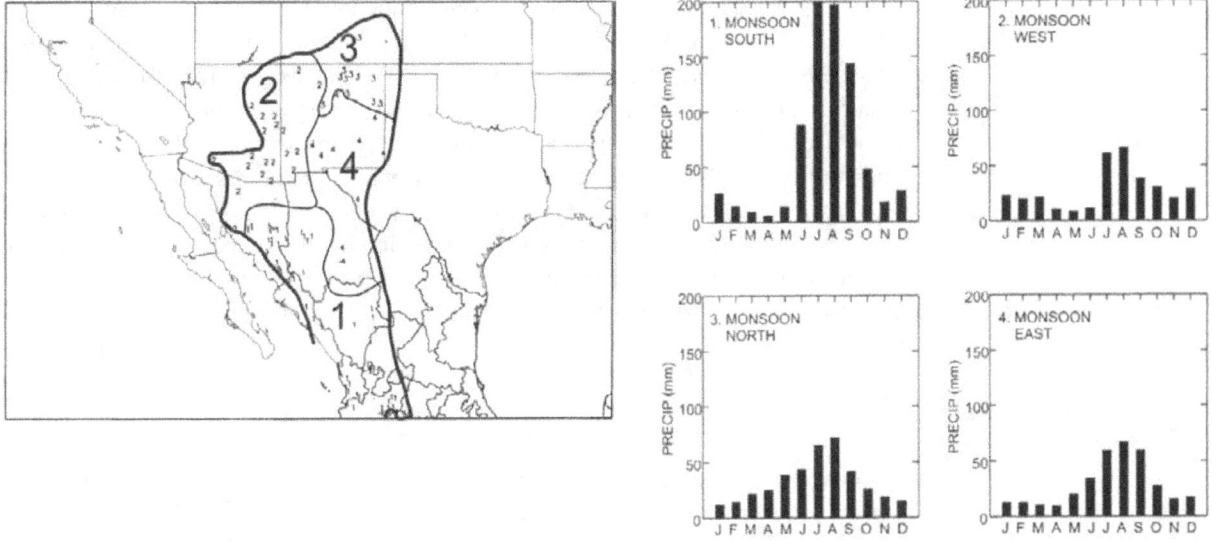

Figure 2. North American monsoon subregions and monthly precipitation patterns. The Barry M. Goldwater Range lies within subregion 2 (Comrie and Glenn 1998).

rains are problematic (Mitchell and others 2002). Of note, however, is that annual monsoon rainfall has historically not been well correlated among the subregions (i.e., a dry summer does not tend to affect all subregions simultaneously), which has important implications for wide ranging and migratory animals.

Water Sources

The Gila River is the major watershed for BMGR-East (INRMP 2003). Upstream areas of the watershed are mostly located on protected lands, so climate change effects on water sources of BMGR-East will primarily be a direct result of changes to precipitation and temperature rather than related to changes in water diversion. Surface water is limited on BMGR-East and mostly ephemeral, and rain catchment basins have been modified in some places to retain water for longer periods (INRMP 2003). Surface water is dependent on local rainfall and thus subject to considerable alteration as climate warms and circulation patterns change. Unfortunately, rainfall is poorly projected, making it difficult to predict changes in natural water sources and run-off, but increasing rainfall variability will almost certainly result in greater interannual variation in the number and longevity of surface water sources. In addition, even with no change in rainfall, predicted higher temperatures will increase evaporation rates, resulting in less moisture available for plants and animals. Similarly, tinajas, where water collects in rock depressions, and other temporary water sources may be threatened.

Disturbance

As the climate changes, greater flood risk from more intense storms is projected for the southwestern United States (Garfin and Lenart 2007; Seager and others 2007). Precipitation falling in intense rainfall events can decrease water available for mesic environments while potentially increasing soil water availability for xeric environments (Knapp and others 2008), which adds to the complexity associated with predicting species' responses to climate change.

Wildfires are expected to become more frequent with projected increases in temperature in many regions (Rogers and Vint 1987; Swetnam and Betancourt 1990; Esser 1992; Westerling and others 2006). Historically, fires in the Sonoran Desert occurred infrequently following periods of high rainfall that produced herbaceous growth capable of carrying fire through usually sparse vegetation (McLaughlin and Bowers 1982). In conjunction with warmer temperatures, projected increases in climate variability will increase fire occurrence as years of high rainfall are followed by dry/hot years, increasing conditions conducive both to ignition and fuel accumulation (McLaughlin and Bowers 1982). Changes in vegetation structure and composition are also important to fire risk and are discussed in Biotic Communities.

Biotic Communities

BMGR-East lies in the center of the Sonoran Desert region. Major plant communities feature various desert scrub communities, including xeroriparian, creosotebush-bursage, and palo-verde mixed cacti. There are also some dune habitats in BMGR-East in the San Cristobal and Growler Valleys (INRMP 2003). Future vegetation will depend on the quantity and season of precipitation, which is not well modeled, as well as the interaction of other factors such as fire, soils, and topography (McPherson and Weltzin 2000).

As temperatures increase, Sonoran Desert boundaries may expand northward and eastward while contracting in the southeast (Weiss and Overpeck 2005). Based on climate modeling of biotic communities, Sonoran desertscrub is expected to remain the dominant biotic community at BMGR-East for at least the next 50 years (Figure 3; Rehfeldt and others 2006). This evidence seems to suggest there will be little change to biotic communities of BMGR-East, but projections lack detail for individual plant species' tolerances, seasonal rainfall, and interacting effects of disturbance that will have major impacts on biodiversity and eventual community composition. Of particular concern for communities in the region is the alteration of bimodal rainfall patterns. Summer rains are not well projected but are particularly important to annuals and succulents, while woody plants tend to rely on winter precipitation (Ehleringer and others 1991). Greater variability in rainfall and increasing droughts will affect xeroriparian communities because water tables will fall with reduced inputs. Palo-verde (*Circidium microphyllum*) is subject to periodic die-offs during droughts with higher mortality with increasing size (Bowers and Turner 2001). Analogous responses and a reduction in trees, particularly in larger size classes, might be expected for similar desert tree species.

Fire regimes in the region have also been altered by introduced plant species that provide fine fuels that carry fire. Spread of invasive plants is of particular concern as they can enhance the spread of fire through sparsely vegetated lands (Brown and Minnich 1986). In particular, grasses, which are primarily C_4, may be favored by increases in temperature and more frequent fire occurrence (Esser 1992). Mediterranean grass (*Schismus barbatus*), a C_4 grass, and Sahara mustard (*Brassica tournefortii*), an annual forb, are common invasives in the region. Sahara mustard germinates following winter rains, has very high germination rates, and can form continuous stands of fuel for fires (Trader and others 2006; Lambert and others 2010). Red brome (*Bromus rubens*) also occurs but is rare on BMGR-East. In addition to competing for water and nutrients, these plants can increase rapidly during wet periods then die back leaving dry, flammable foliage and increased fire risk. Elevated CO_2 can greatly increase productivity of plants where water and nutrients are available (Smith and others 2000). Unfortunately, in arid environments,

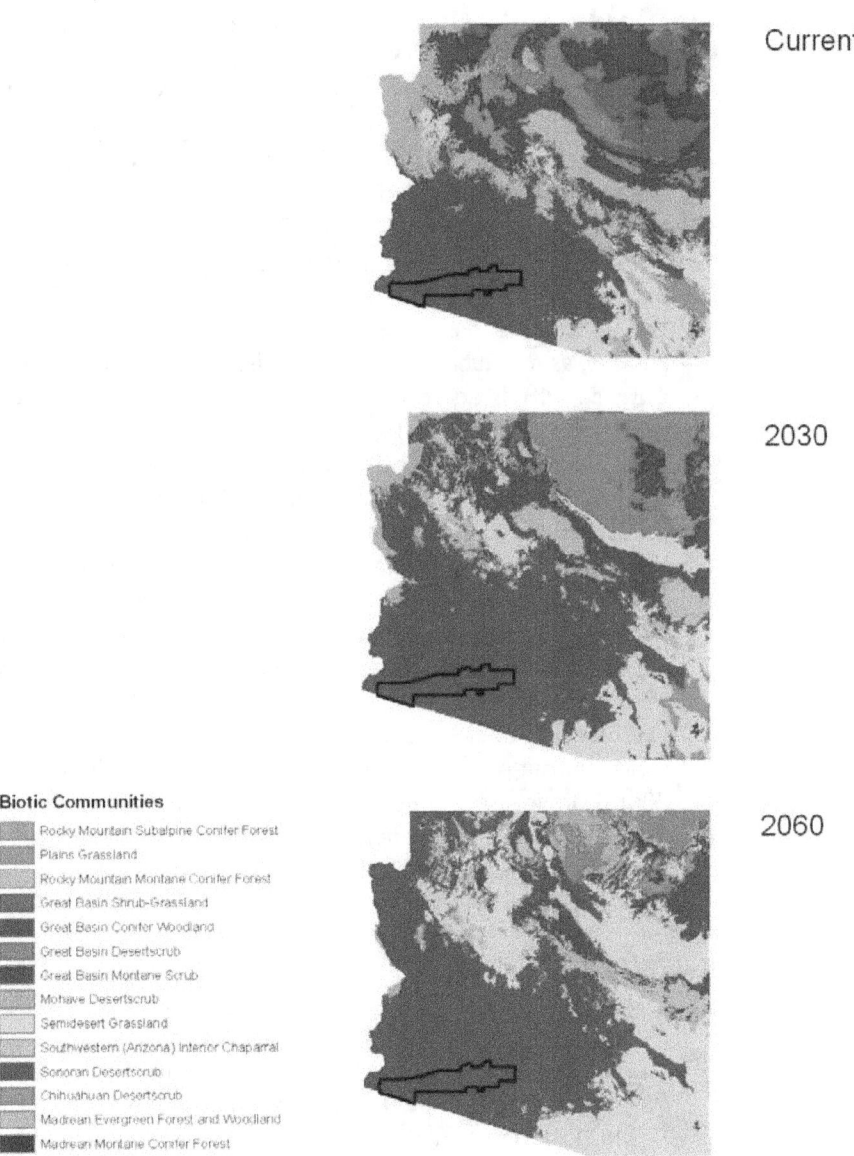

Current

2030

Biotic Communities

Rocky Mountain Subalpine Conifer Forest
Plains Grassland
Rocky Mountain Montane Conifer Forest
Great Basin Shrub-Grassland
Great Basin Conifer Woodland
Great Basin Desertscrub
Great Basin Montane Scrub
Mohave Desertscrub
Semidesert Grassland
Southwestern (Arizona) Interior Chaparral
Sonoran Desertscrub
Chihuahuan Desertscrub
Madrean Evergreen Forest and Woodland
Madrean Montane Conifer Forest

2060

Figure 3. Current and projected climate change as modeled for the biotic communities of Arizona (entire Barry M. Goldwater Range outlined). Projections are from Rehfeldt and others (2006).

this effect of increasing biomass is particularly strong for the non-native red brome during wet years, giving it further competitive advantage over native annuals (Smith and others 2000). Another grass of regional concern that is rapidly expanding and becoming increasingly problematic in the Sonoran Desert is buffelgrass (*Pennisetum ciliare*), a native perennial of Africa introduced for livestock grazing. Buffelgrass promotes a frequent high severity fire regime, which encourages further growth of these grasses while negatively impacting native desert vegetation (Williams and Baruch 2000). Buffelgrass is found throughout the Sonoran Desert region, but at BMGR-East, is known only from a few locations along State Route 85 and the Crater Range (INRMP 2006). It is more extensive to the north along Interstate 8 (Van Devender and Dimmitt 2006).

Many succulent species, particularly cacti, are important elements in the natural communities of BMGR-East. Metabolism (Crassulacean acid metabolism or

CAM) in cacti and other common succulent plants limits water loss by having stomata open at night (Smith and others 1984). Succulents are likely to survive drier conditions, but increases in fires, if they occur, will be detrimental as these plants are often prone to fire mortality. Saguaros (*Carnegiea gigantea*) are long-lived and reproduce episodically with periods of high recruitment that are often followed by periods of decline (Pierson and Turner 1998). Recruitment pulses are also associated with frequent El Niño events, a pattern that is projected to be influenced by warmer temperatures. In general, however, climate is expected to become more variable, thus we expect some years of high moisture to occur that would be favorable to germination. More questionable is the duration of moist periods, as a sequence of wet years is needed for recruitment pulses (Pierson and Turner 1998). In addition, newly recruited seedlings are expected to be vulnerable to drought and intense flooding (Pierson and Turner 1998). Saguaro seedling survival is further reduced by competition with invasive plants, which are expected to increase (Morales-Romero and Molina-Freaner 2008). Cacti phenology is strongly influenced by temperature, and there are clear indications for earlier flowering of many Sonoran desert plant species including columnar and agave cacti (Bowers 2007; Bustamante and Búrquez 2008). In particular, greater variability in fall-winter temperatures is associated with earlier production of flowers, whereas greater variability in mean minimum temperatures is associated with a delay in flowering (Bustamante and Búrquez 2008). Less precipitation and increases in extreme temperatures are likely to shorten the length of flowering season, which has a direct effect on fruit production (as well as nectar availability) (Bustamante and Búrquez 2008). However, warmer winter temperatures will probably extend flowering and fruiting seasons in northern populations near the United States-Mexico border where flowering season is shorter than in more southerly regions (Bustamante and Búrquez 2008).

Mexico and Central America

A few species in this assessment, primarily bats and birds, migrate long distances and are subject to changing climate in regions distant from BMGR-East. Projected changes in pertinent regions are summarized below.

Much of Mexico also has a monsoonal precipitation pattern, but annual rainfall is considerably higher to the south than in the border area near Arizona and New Mexico (Figure 2; Comrie and Glenn 1998). Projecting changes in the climate in Mexico is difficult because many General Circulation Models (GCMs) are unable to adequately describe the current climate. Examining a number of models, it is clear that temperatures will increase for all times of year and most dramatically in northern parts of Mexico. Modeling precipitation is less certain, but most models predict reduced annual and summer rainfall with higher temperatures that will exacerbate drying through evaporation (Liverman and O'Brien 1991). At least currently, monsoons are generally asynchronous between northern-central Mexico and the Southwest borderlands (Comrie and Glenn 1998).

Increases in temperature have also been projected for Central America and, while precipitation projections are again more variable, most models indicate reduced rainfall in wet and dry seasons (Magrin and others 2007). Dry periods are also projected to become more extreme and accompanied by increases in extreme events including intense rain, flooding, and hurricanes (Magrin and others 2007). Central America is also at high risk for forest loss associated with increasing temperatures (Scholze and others 2005). Increases in temperature may lead to conversion of semi-arid regions to arid and the shifting of high-elevation pine and pine-oak forests upslope. Increases in fire, resulting from increased temperatures and more variable rainfall, will reduce some tree species, such as oaks and sycamores, although mature pines should be resistant to all but high severity fires.

Scoring Results and Discussion

Vertebrate Species

Fifteen vertebrate species of BMGR-East were scored for vulnerability to climate change. Full score details and information related to individual species is in Appendix A. The highest score, or the species most vulnerable to population decline, was the Sonoran pronghorn (*Antilocapra americana sonoriensis*) (Figure 4, Table 1). The lowest score was the California leaf-nosed bat (*Macrotus californicus*), although it still had a slightly positive score close to 0, indicating a relatively neutral effect of climate change. Effects on gilded flicker (*Colaptes chrysoides*) were also expected to be relatively neutral overall with few predicted vulnerabilities (Table 2). No species was scored as negative or expected to benefit overall from climate change effects, although many species possessed resilient traits (Table 2). Scores do not directly translate to linear population projections because we do not know the relative importance of each trait in determining population change nor could every possible predictor of population response to climate change be included. Also note that although the highest overall score recorded here, 8.2, is well below the highest possible score of 20, this score would require the species to possess all 22 traits and that each of those traits predicts population decline, which is biologically improbable. The scores are the balance of species' traits associated with vulnerability minus traits associated with resilience; thus, the score indicates the overall predicted direction of change while the magnitude is an indication of how far the balance is skewed toward vulnerable (positive) or resilient (negative) traits.

Figure 4. Sonoran pronghorn was the most vulnerable to climate change of the species scored. This male is marked with an ear tag. Photo by A. Alvidrez.

Table 1. Climate change vulnerability scores for selected vertebrate species at BMGR-East from most vulnerable (positive) to most resilient (negative) scores. Possible scores range from -20 to 20 for overall and -5 to 5 for each category. Uncertainty is a percentage of scoring questions with limited information or contradictory predictions. Full scoring and scientific names are available in Appendix A.

Species	Habitat	Physiology	Phenology	Interactions	**Overall Score**	Uncertainty
Sonoran pronghorn	2.1	1.7	2.5	2.0	8.2	27.0
Morafkai's desert tortoise	2.1	0.5	3.8	1.0	7.0	18.0
Cactus ferruginous pygmy-owl	1.3	0.8	2.5	1.0	5.3	64.0
Yuman fringe-toed lizard	1.4	1.5	0.8	1.0	5.2	27.0
Red-backed whiptail	-0.1	1.7	2.5	1.0	4.4	45.0
American peregrine falcon	-0.1	0.8	2.5	2.0	4.4	18.0
Desert bighorn	-0.1	1.5	2.5	1.0	4.3	32.0
Mexican long-tongued bat	1.3	0.7	0.8	1.0	4.1	27.0
Couch's spadefoot	1.4	-0.3	2.1	1.0	4.1	9.0
Le Conte's thrasher	-0.8	2.5	-0.4	1.0	2.4	36.0
Cave myotis	-1.1	-0.2	3.8	1.0	2.2	32.0
Lesser long-nosed bat	-0.2	0.7	0.8	1.0	2.2	14.0
Saddled leaf-nosed snake	-0.8	-1.0	3.8	1.0	1.5	41.0
Gilded flicker	-0.8	0.8	1.3	0.0	0.8	45.0
California leaf-nosed bat	-0.8	-1.2	3.8	0.0	0.5	36.0

Table 2. Predicted effect of climate change on individual criteria from SAVS designated by shading and letter (n = neutral, v = vulnerable, and r = resilient) for TER-S at BMGR-East. Details on SAVS are found in Bagne and others (2011). Scientific names are in Appendix A.

Species	H1. Changes to Breeding Habitat	H2. Changes to Non-breeding Habitat	H3. Breeding Habitat Components	H4. Non-breeding Habitat Components	H5. Changes to Habitat Quality	H6. Dispersal ability	H7. Migration Habitats	PS1. Limiting Physiological Conditions	PS2. Temperature-determined Sex Ratios	PS3. Disturbance Events	PS4. Daily Activity Period	PS5. Adaptive Strategies	PS6. Metabolic Rate	PH1. Reliance on Climate Cues	PH2. Reliance on Discrete Resource Peaks	PH3. Activities and Resource Separation	PH4. # of Reproductive Events per Year	I1. Changes in Food Resources	I2. Changes in Predation	I3. Symbiotic Relationships	I4. Changes in Disease	I5. Changes in Competition
Sonoran pronghorn	n	n	n	v	v	v	n	v	n	n	n	v	n	n	v	n	v	v	n	n	v	n
Morafka's desert tortoise	n	n	n	v	v	v	n	v	n	n	n	r	n	v	v	n	v	n	n	n	n	n
Cactus ferruginous pygmy-owl	v	v	n	n	v	r	n	v	v	n	v	n	r	n	v	n	r	v	n	n	n	v
Yuman fringe-toed lizard	n	n	n	v	n	v	n	v	n	n	n	n	n	v	v	n	v	n	n	v	n	v
Red-backed whiptail	n	n	n	n	v	r	n	v	n	n	v	v	r	n	v	n	r	v	n	n	n	n
American peregrine falcon	n	n	n	n	n	r	v	n	n	n	n	v	n	n	v	n	v	v	n	n	v	n
Desert bighorn	n	n	n	n	v	r	n	n	n	n	n	r	n	n	v	n	v	n	n	n	v	n
Mexican long-tongued bat	v	v	n	n	n	r	v	r	n	n	n	v	n	n	v	r	v	v	n	n	n	n
Couch's spadefoot	n	n	v	n	v	n	n	v	n	n	v	r	r	v	v	r	v	v	n	n	n	n
Le Conte's thrasher	n	n	n	n	n	r	n	v	n	n	v	n	n	n	v	n	v	v	n	n	n	n
Cave myotis	r	r	n	n	v	r	n	v	n	n	n	r	n	n	v	v	r	n	n	n	v	n
Lesser long-nosed bat	n	v	n	n	r	r	v	r	n	v	n	v	n	n	v	r	v	v	n	n	n	n
Saddled leaf-nosed snake	n	n	n	n	n	r	n	n	n	n	n	n	r	v	v	n	v	v	n	n	n	n
Gilded flicker	n	n	n	n	n	r	n	n	n	n	n	v	n	n	n	n	v	n	n	n	n	n
California leaf-nosed bat	n	n	n	n	n	r	n	r	n	r	n	v	n	n	v	v	v	n	n	n	n	n

Examination of the category scores reveals more details on vulnerability (Table 1). Note that category scores are adjusted to be on a comparable scale because a different number of questions comprise each category. This adjustment is not made for overall scores where each question is of equal weight regardless of category. In this set of scores, a low overall score may be a result of neutral effects across several categories (i.e., few vulnerabilities) or a combination of vulnerable traits balanced by resilient traits, such as for the California leaf-nosed bat (Table 2). This has important implications for management and is critical to score interpretation because the relative influence of individual traits on populations is unknown.

Phenology was consistently an important category in vulnerability for most species (Table 1). The phenology category score reflects the relative influence of climate on species' phenology, timing of resources, and the potential for timing flexibility. The majority of species had phenological vulnerabilities from critical timing tied to discrete resource peaks and inflexibility in reproductive events to provide resilience to those timing changes (Table 2). Ultimate outcome of these relationships is difficult to project because synchronicity of species to resources can depend on the degree of timing shifts from multiple elements. Absence of favorable timing predictions is partly due to the lack of knowledge about cues and temporal resources for many species, but we also know that timing is sensitive to warming and has already been detected in a broad range of species (Bradley and others 1999; Jenni and Kery 2003; Millar and Herdman 2004). Interactions tended to have neutral scores, but uncertainty was also high for this category as information on key biological interactions is often limited (Appendix A). Habitat was an important vulnerability category for several of the most vulnerable species despite the prediction of resilience of the dominant vegetation type, Sonoran desert scrub, in this region (Table 1 and Table 2). Predictions of habitat change based solely on biome shifts do not entirely capture habitat-related vulnerability and may be inadequate to use as a proxy for changes in associated species. Dispersal ability, another of the habitat scoring criteria, was an important area of resilience for a majority of species; thus, minimizing dispersal barriers will be important (Table 2).

All species scored were vulnerable rather than resilient to climate change overall. It is likely that this result is partly due to climate change exacerbating current stressors that are already responsible for declines in these species. Additionally, exposure or the magnitude of climate change is expected to be high in the Southwest, increasing vulnerability of species in the region. Although the calculation of scores is such that possible negative and positive scores are equal, there could be some other bias in scoring, such as a tendency of the scorer to favor vulnerability scores or some inherent factor in the system that biases it toward vulnerable (positive) scores. There was no clear link between uncertainty and vulnerability score, thus there was no obvious bias related to incomplete information (Table 1).

All taxonomic classes had similar average vulnerability with the lowest for birds (average = 3.2) and the highest for reptiles (average = 4.5). Members of these groups do not cluster together but are scattered throughout the rankings. The most vulnerable species, the Sonoran pronghorn, is also an endangered species, although the other endangered species, the lesser long-nosed bat (*Leptonycteris yerbabuenae*), was relatively less vulnerable than most other species in the assessment. Importantly, the two species under review by USFWS for listing—Sonoran populations of the desert tortoise (now Morafkai's desert tortoise) and Arizona populations of the cactus ferruginous pygmy-owl (*Glaucidium brasilianum cactorum*)—are also the second and third most vulnerable in this assessment. These species were also more vulnerable than resilient across all categories (Figure 5). The scope of this assessment may be partly responsible for these patterns.

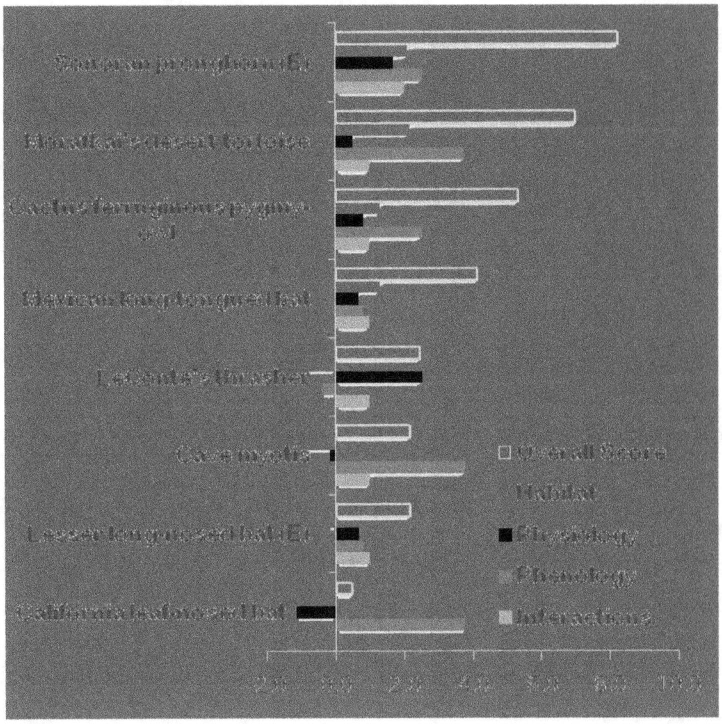

Figure 5. Vulnerability category and overall scores for endangered species (E), Federal candidate species, or Federal species of concern at BMGR-East. Scientific names appear in Appendix A.

Vascular Plants

Only one plant species was assessed, the acuña cactus (*Echinomastus erectrocentrus* var. *acunensis*). It is a USFWS candidate for listing. It received a vulnerability score of 2.8 out of a maximum of 10, indicating increased vulnerability to population declines with projected climate change. The category scores, each with a maximum of 3, are 1.5 for habitat, -1.0 for physiology, and 2.0 for interactions. That a cactus species is also vulnerable to declines associated with climate change despite physiological adaptations to hot climates is an important outcome for management. Interactions such as fire and invasive plants may threaten habitats and pollinators or seed dispersal may be reduced if associated species decline or shift migration timing out of sync with the flowering phenology of the cactus.

Management Implications: Using Assessment Results

This assessment seeks to help clarify the threat of climate change to individual species and identify potential management actions. Management of TER-S, however, is not exclusively based on vulnerability, nor is climate change the only potential threat to species. Feasibility, economics, and political considerations all play a role in management decisions, but are outside the scope of this assessment. Other aspects of prioritization such as population trends or genetic uniqueness are also considerations (Given and Norton 1993). Management actions are likely to be more effective and targeted if priorities and potential impacts are clear.

During scoring, we kept our focus on the coming decades that, while more conservative than longer outlooks, are of more practical use to current management and are more projectable. Below, we summarize management themes gleaned from the individual species accounts, which contain detailed information for each species (see Appendix A). These themes suggested target areas for management

Table 3. Summary of common management target areas for reducing anticipated climate change threats to individual species on BMGR-East. This list is not comprehensive but includes areas that were shared by multiple species and that have the potential to reduce climate change vulnerability. Specific management actions may differ for species within the same target area. "Timing restrictions" refers to altering dates when activities are restricted. Options marked "(x)" may have response to management in the opposite direction to other species. Scientific names appear in Appendix A.

Species	Fire/Invasive Plants	Water sources	Vehicular traffic	Shade and microsites	Corridors and dispersal	Timing restrictions
Sonoran pronghorn	x	x		x	x	x
Morafkai's desert tortoise	x	x	x	x	x	
Cactus ferruginous pygmy-owl	x					x
Yuman fringe-toed lizard			x	x	x	
Red-backed whiptail	x			x		
American peregrine falcon		x				x
Desert bighorn	x	x				x
Mexican long-tongued bat	x					x
Couch's spadefoot		x	x		x	x
Le Conte's thrasher	x	(x)	x	x		x
Cave myotis		x				x
Lesser long-nosed bat	x					x
Saddled leaf-nosed snake			x			
Gilded flicker	x					
California leaf-nosed bat						x
Acuña cactus	x			x		

that were common to multiple species (Table 3). For example, vulnerability related to heat tolerance may be mitigated through managing for plants that provide shade or by providing drinking water sources. Habitats threatened by increased fire may be protected by removing invasive plants or creating fire breaks. Often called adaptation strategies, these actions reduce the impacts of climate change or increase resilience of species or their habitats. Other management strategies may focus on reducing current threats to species, including those that may be exacerbated by climate change such as water withdrawals, border traffic, and energy development. Management implications are general recommendations from the assessment that should be considered for species management and not as a critique of current management programs.

Artificial and Natural Waters

Artificial waters are widely used in wildlife management in the Southwest, although the benefits and potential negative impacts are not well quantified (Broyles 1995). Regardless, increasing droughts and high temperatures will likely make these water sources critical to many species as water requirements increase. This situation may also apply to species that can usually satisfy most of their water needs through diet when faced with more extreme conditions. The majority of modified natural water catchments on BMGR-East are located in the Sand Tank and Sauceda Mountains (INRMP 2003). Current and proposed natural and artificial waters on BMGR-East, including valley locations, should be evaluated for availability to a wide variety of species under drought conditions. Rosenstock and others (2004) provided detailed analysis and recommendations for water enhancements. Evaluation of future suitability of water enhancements should pay particular attention to substrates, capacity and annual longevity, habitat surroundings, special species requirements, disease transmission, and potential for supplemental water inputs. Accordingly, artificial waters may need to be expanded or modified.

Fire, Fuels, and Invasive Species Management

As previously described, conditions conducive to fire ignition and spread are expected to increase. Because individual species respond differently to fire, fires that burn very large areas or encourage conversion to non-native vegetation are of the most concern from a biodiversity perspective. Xeroriparian habitats, for example, may be more vulnerable as the denser vegetation provides more fuel for fires. Of particular concern in this region is the interplay between climate, fire, and invasive species, which could degrade habitats for a wide variety of species (Figure 6).

Management of non-native plants, rather than fuel management, will be key as a number of non-native plants play a major role in altering fire regimes and can outcompete native grasses and forbs. Measures that prevent introductions and spread will be essential and less costly than control measures after non-natives have become established. Critical areas for control may include locations of known TER-S or adjacent to habitats with TER-S, dispersal sources such as along roads, and areas with increased ignition risk. Elevated CO_2 may also exacerbate competitive dominance of non-natives, particularly during wet years, and managers should anticipate annual variability in the need for invasive species control measures. Increasing drought periods, however, may reduce red brome and other invasives that lack persistent seed banks and can present opportunities for effective control (Burgess and others 1991; Salo 2004).

Anticipating Shifts in Distribution

Depending on a wide variety of factors, including dispersal ability, physiological thresholds, and vegetation response, populations may shift in distribution as local climate changes. From the perspective of a management unit, these shifts will be observed as a change in numbers regardless of the greater population. Management efforts will be better spent on species that are less able to shift with changing habitats than on those that are disappearing from BMGR-East but increasing elsewhere. Shifting of habitats or populations should also be anticipated for geographically based protected areas or designated critical habitat. Managers

Figure 6. Species like the desert tortoise are vulnerable to loss of habitat, including loss of cactus, an important food and water source, and shrubs that provide shade. Increases in invasive grasses and frequency of fires will accelerate habitat change. Photo by D. Garcia.

will need to reevaluate the future suitability of current or proposed protected areas. Drier or more variable conditions may shift timing and locations of foraging habitats for species like the Sonoran pronghorn or the lesser long-nosed bat. Although we did not assess species that do not occur at BMGR-East, new species may disperse to the region that require inclusion in management planning. We anticipate some migratory species limited by cold winter conditions to increase use of BMGR-East toward year-round residency. Summer conditions will likely limit expansion of new species into the region that are not already tolerant of high temperatures. Monitoring can help identify species in the early stages of expansion.

Movements and migrations are partly adaptations to changing conditions, thus species may reduce vulnerability by shifting with climate. To facilitate population shifts, corridors will be an important part of managing species under climate change. Of particular concern are the highway barriers that prevent some species from moving to the more mesic environments of the Gila River and Río Sonoyta. These movements are likely critical during drought periods for individual survival. This conditional migration is particularly relevant to sustaining Sonoran pronghorn populations.

It may be necessary in some cases to assist the migration process to prevent extinction. Generally known as assisted migration, individuals are moved to new, presumably favorable locations outside of their historic range. Costs can be high, and the nature of climate change is such that new locations cannot be expected to remain suitable in the long term. Introduction of species to new regions is also fraught with problems, including disruption of species interactions, hybridization, and unpredictable outcomes (Ricciardi and Simberloff 2009). Translocations that include recent historical range (i.e., reintroductions) eliminate many of these issues, but may be of questionable benefit in the long term as the climate continues to warm. Conversely, translocations may be beneficial for climate change management as new locations may include more favorable microsites, help reduce the risk of stochastic events, offer better natural dispersal opportunities, or buy time until further actions can be evaluated. Falk and others (1996) provided guidelines for rare plant reintroductions.

Coping With Physiological Thresholds

Although physiological limitations may shift species' distributions, limitations will also add to stress manifested as poor survival or reproduction (Bernardo and Spotila 2006). On initial consideration, desert species might be expected to be resilient to increasing heat and aridity, which are the conditions they are adapted to. This idea ignores the relatively narrow window of adaptation available at the upper physiological thresholds that may make species in extreme environments more rather than less vulnerable (Pörtner 2001; Stillman 2003; Hargrove 2010; Sinervo and others 2010). TER-S are at a particular disadvantage for physiological stress, as their small population size will limit adaptation through natural selection. In addition, little is known about physiological tolerances of species under projected future conditions. In this assessment, we assumed tolerances would be exceeded for those species already prone to drought mortality or inhabiting the most extreme environments, but this topic needs more study and will be dependent on future greenhouse gas emission rates.

Although an entire management area can become physiologically unsuitable, it is likely that some favorable microsites will remain, at least for the near future. Besides the management of artificial and natural waters already discussed, managers can take advantage of variation in environmental conditions across the landscape and direct protection or enhancements to favorable microsites. In this assessment, limitations of high heat or low moisture were the most concerning, thus priority could be given to microsites with suitable habitat that are cool and moist, such as north-facing slopes or canyon bottoms. Microsites that provide shade are important to thermoregulation (Walsberg 1993) and management that encourages shade plants could be of benefit to some species. Xeroriparian areas are important for a number of TER-S as well as migrating bird species and likely provide important thermal refuges from the more sparse and exposed adjacent vegetation. Managers should also note that more mesic microsites and shaded areas are also more prone to invasion by non-native annuals (Brooks 1999). In addition, because drought is a limiting factor for many of these species, managers should include drought effects in planning documents and anticipate the possible need for intervention.

Anticipating Shifts in Timing

Phenology is an important aspect of life history and is often sensitive to climate conditions. It also was the category most associated with vulnerability for vertebrate species in this assessment (Table 1) and is a potential issue for plant species that are pollinated or dispersed by animals. Management that is time sensitive, such as restricting activities during breeding of a target species, needs to anticipate that timing will change and restrictions must track those changes. Although timing of individuals is not readily managed, in some cases, management can affect the timing of resources, such as the presence and duration of temporary pools.

Prioritization

The apparent vulnerability of most TER-S on BMGR-East to climate change highlights the challenges that will face managers and the need for proactive solutions. Managers already make choices about where to focus resources, but as stresses on species magnify, there will likely be an increasing need to prioritize species and/or actions. Identification of vulnerabilities suggests target areas for effective management, some of which can affect multiple species (Table 3). Scores from this assessment can be used to aid decisions by identifying species most vulnerable to the additional impact of climate change and the species' traits associated with vulnerabilities. Species that are expected to be resilient may require management if they negatively impact TER-S. Ranks in this assessment are based on the number of predicted vulnerabilities across species for the same set of criteria, but likely do not directly translate to a linear progression of population change because some traits may have threshold effects or may be limiting factors. Obviously, predictions of climate and vulnerability are uncertain, but an assessment, even if limited, can provide input when no other information is available and serve as a starting point for beginning to address species management under climate change.

Landscape-Scale Management and Partners

Perhaps one of the greatest challenges for managing species under future climate is that with continued greenhouse gas emissions, the future is not a steady state. Most management planning, however, focuses on the next 10 to 20 years and we assessed species with that timeline in mind. Partners will be extremely valuable, and managers from adjacent lands will be experiencing similar climate conditions and issues. Management at a landscape scale is well suited for climate change issues, as well as being cost effective. Cooperative approaches can allow more flexibility and help to balance the costs and benefits of competing needs. For example, cooperative monitoring at a large scale can separate population shifts from regional declines and detect newly arriving species early. Natural variability in local conditions at a landscape scale will also be important for many aspects of species' responses to climate as identified here. For example, temperature variation across a broad landscape may help ensure variation in population sex ratios for species such as desert tortoise. BMGR-East is well situated for landscape-scale management; in addition to comprising a large geographic area, it is surrounded by large, undeveloped public and tribal lands.

Uncertainty

Although drawn from basic life history and ecology, in many instances, uncertainty arose during the scoring process because of lack of information. Deficiencies were common in a few key areas for vertebrates, but were more extensive for plant species and ultimately limited the scoring criteria available. Lack of information was doubly problematic for interactions as few key interacting species (e.g., prey, predators, pollinators, and disease vectors) were known, nor were there often climate change projections for these species. Despite limitations in prediction, we felt it was important to include critical relationships of species with climate. Uncertainties were used to identify research priorities, which are noted in the individual species accounts (Appendix A). Predicting the future is inherently uncertain, but the exercise of prediction will improve as better models are developed and more research is conducted.

Next Steps

Vulnerability and resilience predictions are based on responses that are likely a matter of degree and are dependent on the strength or duration of projected changes. This assessment is not meant to substitute for more thorough and complex analyses of the climate change response of individual species, but those approaches will also be limited in their ability to predict the future. Predictions for plant species were particularly difficult to make using this approach and may be more suitable for modeling techniques based on climate envelope or niche modeling than vertebrate species. The scoring systems used in this assessment are simple and flexible by design. Scores can easily be modified to reflect any future changes in projections, although we suspect these will make little difference to the outcome. Managers are encouraged to apply scoring to additional species or to use their knowledge to modify the scoring of species included here. By focusing on ecology and life history traits, these scoring systems can take advantage of the considerable knowledge of local resource managers rather than depend on expertise in modeling or computer simulations that need to be tailored to particular species or regions.

This assessment can help identify management targets, including species and actions. Information from assessments can also be used as part of more complex multi-species or landscape planning such as outlined by Lawson and others (2008). In addition, this assessment highlights different pathways by which populations can be affected by climate, which is important for initiating dialogue and finding solutions. Predicting effects on individual species is inherently complex and primarily speculative at this point, but we believe that the need for managers to address climate change is becoming more urgent (Thomas and others 2004) and tools, regardless of their limitations, are needed now. We also want to emphasize that managing for climate change is not just about challenges, but also about opportunities (Box 2). While the assessment process and the product are inherently imprecise, this effort is an important first step toward anticipating and responding to climate change, and it provides a framework for integrating new research and information.

Box 2. Seizing Opportunity

Although climate change will present challenges to species and their management, opportunites will likely be presented as well. The shifting of species distributions can mean a local reduction in an undesirable species, such as an alien plant species (Bradley 2009), or an improvement for a new species, such as a species that shifts its distribution from a degraded habitat to a protected area. Natural resource managers can take advantage of increasing climate variability to implement actions during the most favorable conditions. For example, drought in arid systems can sometimes favor native species over non-native species, assisting weed control (Salo 2004). During wet periods, planting or natural recruitment in combination with grazing may improve seedling establishment of woody species (Holmgren and Sheffer 2001). Translocation or corridor enhancements to encourage animal dispersal may be most successful during wet years associated with high reproductive success. The climate change challenge may also serve as a catalyst to promote adaptive management strategies, highlight sustainability, and foster partnerships.

Literature Cited

Arizona Game and Fish Department (AGFD). 2006. DRAFT. Arizona's comprehensive wildlife conservation strategy: 2005-2015. Arizona Game and Fish Department, Phoenix, Arizona.

Archer, S. R. and K. I. Predick. 2008. Climate change and ecosystems of the southwestern United States. Rangelands 30:23-28.

Arriaga, L., A. E. Castellanos, E. Moreno, and J. Alarcon. 2004. Potential ecological distribution of alien invasive species and risk assessment: a case study of buffel grass in arid regions of Mexico. Conservation Biology 18:1504-1514.

Bagne, K. E., M. M. Friggens, and D. M. Finch. 2011. A system for assessing vulnerability of species (SAVS) to climate change. USDA Forest Service, Rocky Mountain Research Station, Gen. Tech. Rep. RMRS-GTR-257. Online at: http://www.fs.fed.us/rm/grassland-shrubland-desert/products/species-vulnerability/savs-climate-change-tool.

Bernardo, J. and J. Spotila. 2006. Physiological constraints on organismal response to global warming: mechanistic insights from clinally varying populations and implications for assessing endangerment. Biology Letters 2:135-139.

Bowers, J. E. and R. M. Taylor. 2001. Dieback and episodic mortality of *Cercidium microphyllum* (foothill paloverde), a dominant Sonoran Desert tree. Journal of the Torrey Botanical Society 128:128-140.

Bradley, N. L., A. C. Leopold, J. Ross, and W. Huffaker. 1999. Phenological changes reflect climate change in Wisconsin. Proceedings of the National Academy of Sciences of the United States of America 96:9701-9704.

Brooks, M. L. 1999. Habitat invasibility and dominance by alien annual plants in the western Mojave Desert. Biological Invasions 1:325-337.

Brown, D. E., and R. A. Minnich. 1986. Fire and changes in creosote bush scrub of the western Sonoran desert, California. American Midland Naturalist 116:411-422.

Broyles, B. 1995. Desert wildlife water developments: questioning use in the Southwest. Wildlife Society Bulletin 23:663-675.

Burgess, T. L., J. E. Bowers, and R. M. Turner. 1991. Exotic plants at the desert laboratory, Tucson, Arizona. Madroño 38:96-114.

Burquez-Montijo, A., M. Miller, and A. Martinez-Yrizar. 2002. Mexican grasslands, thornscrub, and the transformation of the Sonoran Desert by invasive exotic buffelgrass. Pages 126-146 In B. Tellman, ed., Arizona-Sonoran Desert Museum Studies in Natural History, Tucson, AZ.

Comrie, A. C. and E. C. Glenn. 1998. Principal components-based regionalization of precipitation regimes across southwest United States and northern Mexico, with an application to monsoon precipitation variability. Climate Research 10:201-215.

Cook, E. R., R. Seager, R. R. Heim, Jr., R. S. Vose, C. Herweijer, and C. Woodhouse. 2009. Megadroughts in North America: placing IPCC projections of hydroclimatic change in a long-term palaeoclimate context. Journal of Quaternary Science 25:48-61.

Early, R. and D. F. Sax. 2011. Analysis of climate paths reveals potential limitations on species range shifts. Ecology Letters 14:1125-1133.

Esser, Gerd. 1992. Implications of climate change for production and decomposition in grasslands and coniferous forests. Ecological Applications 2:47-54.

Falk, D., C. Millar, and M. Olwell. 1996. Part Five: Guidelines for Preparing a Rare Plant Reintroduction Plan. Pages 454-490 In D. Falk, C. Millar, and M. Olwell, eds., Restoring Diversity: Strategies for Reintroduction of Endangered Plants. Island Press, Washington, DC.

Field, C. B., L. D. Mortsch, M. Brklacich, D. L. Forbes, P. Kovacs, J. A. Patz, S. W. Running, and M. J. Scott. 2007. North America. Pages 617-652 In M. L. Parry, O. F. Canziani, J. P. Palutikof, P. J. van der Linden and C. E. Hanson, eds., Climate Change 2007: Impacts, Adaptation and Vulnerability. Contribution of Working Group II to the Fourth Assessment Report of the Intergovernmental Panel on Climate Change. Cambridge University Press, Cambridge, UK.

Garfin, G. and M. Lenart. 2007. Climate change effects on Southwest water resources. Southwest Hydrology 6:16-17.

Given, D. R. and D. A. Norton. 1993. A multivariate approach to assessing threat and priority setting in threatened species conservation. Biological Conservation 64:57-66.

Glick, P., B. A. Stein, N. A. Edelson, eds. 2011. Scanning the Conservation Horizon: A Guide to Climate Change Vulnerability Assessment. National Wildlife Federation, Washington, DC.

Graham, E. A. and P. S. Nobel. 1996. Long term effects of a doubled atmospheric CO_2 concentration on the CAM species *Agave deserti*. Journal of Experimental Botany 47:61-69.

Graham, R. T., S. McCaffrey, and T. B. Jain, tech. eds. 2004. Science basis for changing forest structure to modify wildfire behavior and severity. Gen. Tech. Rep. RMRS-GTR-120. Fort Collins, CO: U.S. Department of Agriculture, Forest Service, Rocky Mountain Research Station. 43 p.

Hall, J. A., P. Comer, A. Gondor, R. Marshall, and S. Weinstein. 2001. Conservation Elements of and a Biodiversity Management Framework for the Barry M. Goldwater Range, Arizona. The Nature Conservancy of Arizona, Tucson.

Hargrove, L. J. 2010. Limits to species' distributions: spatial structure and dynamics of breeding bird populations along an ecological gradient. Dissertation. University of California, Riverside, CA.

Holmgren, M. and M. Scheffer. 2001. El Niño as a window of opportunity for the restoration of degraded arid ecosystems. Ecosystems 4:151-159.

Integrated Natural Resources Management Plan (INRMP). 2003. Final environmental impact statement for Barry M. Goldwater Range: volume I. U.S. Department of the Air Force, U.S. Department of the Navy, U.S. Department of the Interior, and Arizona Game and Fish Department.

Jenni, L. and M. Kéry. 2003. Timing of autumn bird migration under climate change: advances in long-distance migrants, delays in short-distance migrants. Proceedings of the Royal Society 270:1467-1471.

Kelly, A. and M. Goulden. 2008. Rapid shifts in plant distribution with recent climate change. Proceedings of the National Academy of Sciences USA 105:11823-11826.

Knapp, A. K., C. Beier, D. D. Briske, [and others]. 2008. Consequences of more extreme precipitation regimes for terrestrial ecosystems. Bioscience 58:811-821.

Lambert, A., C. D'Antonio, and T. Dudley. 2010. Invasive species and fire in California ecosystems. Fremontia 38:29:36.

Lawson, D., H. Regan, and T. Mizerek. 2008. Multi-species management using modeling and decision theory: applications to integrated natural resources management planning. DoD Legacy Program Report, Project 05-264.

Lenoir, J. J., C. Gegout, P. A. Marquet, P. de Ruffray, and H. Brisse. 2008. A significant upward shift in plant species optimum elevation during the 20th century. Science 320:1768-1771.

Liverman, D. M. and K. L. O'Brien. 1991. Global warming and climate change in Mexico. Pages 351-364 In Global Environmental Change. Butterworth-Heinemann Ltd.

Lucier, A., M. Palmer, H. Mooney, K. Nadelhoffer, D. Ojima, and F. Chavez. 2006. Ecosystems and climate change: research priorities for the U.S. Climate Change Science Program. Recommendations from the scientific community. Report on an ecosystems workshop, prepared for the Ecosystems Interagency Working Group. Special Series No. SS-92-06, University of Maryland Center for Environmental Science, Chesapeake Biological Laboratory, Solomons, MD. 50 p.

Magrin, G., C. Gay García, D. Cruz Choque, J. C. Giménez, A. R. Moreno, G. J. Nagy, C. Nobre and A. Villamizar. 2007. Latin America. In M.L. Parry, O.F. Canziani, J.P. Palutikof, P.J. van der Linden and C.E. Hanson, eds., Climate Change 2007: Impacts, Adaptation and Vulnerability. Contribution of Working Group II to the Fourth Assessment Report of the Intergovernmental Panel on Climate Change. Cambridge University Press, Cambridge, UK: 581-615.

Maurer, E. P., L. Brekke, T. Pruitt, and P. B. Duffy. 2007. Fine-resolution climate projections enhance regional climate change impact studies, Eos Trans. AGU 88:504.

McLaughlin, J. F., J. J. Hellmann, C. L. Boggs, and P. R. Ehrlich. 2002. Climate change hastens population extinctions. Proceedings of the National Academy of Sciences 99:6070-6074.

McLaughlin, S. E. and J. P. Bowers. 1982. Effects of wildfire on a Sonoran Desert plant community. Ecology 63:246-248.

McPherson, G. R. and J. F. Weltzin. 2000. Disturbance and climate change in United States/Mexico borderland plant communities: a state-of-the-knowledge review. USDA Forest Service, Gen. Tech. Rep. RMRS-GTR-50.

Millar, J. and E. Herdman. 2004. Climate change and the initiation of spring breeding by deer mice in the Kananaskis Valley, 1985-2003. Canadian Journal of Zoology 82:1444-1450.

Minnich, R. A. and Y. H. Chou. 1997. Wildland fire patch dynamics in the Chaparral of southern California and northern Baja California. International Journal of Wildland Fire 7:221-248.

Mitchell, D. L., D. Ivanova, R. Rabin, K. Redmond, and T. J. Brown. 2002. Gulf of California sea surface temperatures and the North American monsoon: mechanistic implications from observations. Journal of Climate 15:2261-2281.

Morales-Romero, D. and F. Molina-Freaner. 2008. Influence of buffelgrass pasture conversion on the regeneration and reproduction of the columnar cactus, *Pachycereus pecten-aboriginum*, in northwestern Mexico. Journal of Arid Environments 72:228-237.

NatureServe. 2004. Species at risk on Department of Defense installations: revised report and documentation. Report (Legacy 03-154) prepared for Department of Defense and U.S. Fish and Wildlife Service.

Pierson, E. and R. Turner. 1998. An 85-year study of Saguaro (*Carnegiea gigantea*) demography. Ecology 79:2676-2693.

Pörtner, H. O. 2001. Climate change and temperature-dependent biogeography: oxygen limitation of thermal tolerance in animals. Naturwissenschaften 88:137-146.

Rehfeldt, G. E., N. L. Crookston, M. V. Warwell, and J. S. Evans. 2006. Empirical analyses of plant-climate relationships for the western United States. International Journal of Plant Sciences 167:1123-1150.

Ricciardi, A. and D. Simberloff. 2009. Assisted colonization is not a viable conservation strategy. Trends in Ecology and Evolution 24:248-253.

Richter, B., R. Mathews, D. Harrison, and R. Wigington. 2003. Ecologically sustainable water management: managing river flows for ecological integrity. Ecological Applications 13:206-224.

Robinett, D. 1994. Fire effects on southeastern Arizona Plains grasslands. Rangelands 16:143-148.

Rogers, G. F. and M. K. Vint. 1987. Winter precipitation and fire in the Sonoran Desert. Journal of Arid Environments 13:47-52.

Rojas-Martinez, A., A. Valiente-Banuet, M. del Coro Arizmendi, A. Alcantara-Eguren, and H. T. Arita. 1999. Seasonal distribution of the long-nosed bat (*Leptonycteris curasoae*) in North America: does a generalized migration pattern really exist? Journal of Biogeography 26:1065-1077.

Rosenstock, S. S., M. J. Rabe, C. S. O'Brien, and R. B. Waddell. 2004. Studies of wildlife water developments in southwestern Arizona: wildlife use, water quality, wildlife diseases, wildlife mortalities, and influences on native pollinators. Arizona Game and Fish Department, Research Branch Technical Guidance Bulletin No. 8, Phoenix. 15 p.

Salo, L. F. 2004. Population dynamics of red brome (*Bromus madritensis* subsp. *rubens*): times for concern, opportunities for management. Journal of Arid Environments 57:291-296.

Scholze, M., W. Knorr, N. W. Arnell and I. C. Prentice. 2005. A climate change risk analysis for world ecosystems. Proceedings of the National Academy of Sciences 103:13116-13120.

Seager, R., T. Ming, I. Held, [and others]. 2007. Model projections of an imminent transition to a more arid climate in southwestern North America. Science 316:1181-1184.

Serrat-Capdevila, A., J. B. Valdes, J. G. Perez, K. Baird, L. J. Mata, and T. Maddock. 2007. Modeling climate change impacts and uncertainty on the hydrology of a riparian system: the San Pedro Basin (Arizona/Sonora). Journal of Hydrology 347:48-66.

Shepperd, P., A. Comrie, G. Packin, K. Angersbach, and M. Hughs. 2002. The climate of the US Southwest. Climate Research 21:219-238.

Sinervo, B., F. Méndez-de-la-Cruz, D. B. Miles, [and others]. 2010. Erosion of lizard diversity by climate change and altered thermal niches. Science 328:894-899.

Smith, S. D., B. Didden-Zopfy and P. S. Nobel. 1984. High-temperature responses of North American cacti. Ecology 65:643-651.

Smith, Stanley D., Travis E. Huxman, Stephen F. Zitzer, Therese N. Charlet, David C. Housman, James S. Coleman, Lynn K. Fenstermaker, Jeffrey R. Seemann, and Robert S. Nowak. 2000. Elevated CO_2 increases productivity and invasive species success in an arid ecosystem. Nature 408:79-82.

Stephens, S. L. and L. W. Ruth. 2005. Federal forest-fire policy in the United States. Ecological Applications 15:532-542.

Stillman, J. H. 2003. Acclimation capacity underlies susceptibility to climate change. Science 301:65.

Stromberg, J. C. 1998. Dynamics of Fremont cottonwood (*Populus fremontii*) and saltcedar (*Tamarix chinensis*) populations along the San Pedro River, Arizona. Journal of Arid Environments 40:133-155.

Stromberg, J. C., S. J. Lite, T. J. Rychener, L. Levick, M. D. Dixon, and J. W. Watts. 2006. Status of the riparian ecosystem in the upper San Pedro River, Arizona: Application of an assessment model. Environmental Monitoring and Assessment 115:145-173.

Stromberg, J. C., R. Tiller, and B. Richter. 1996. Effects of groundwater decline on riparian vegetation of semiarid regions: the San Pedro, Arizona. Ecological Applications 6:113-131.

Swetnam, T. W. and Betancourt, J. L. 1990. Fire-Southern Oscillation relations in the southwestern United States. Science 249:1017-1021.

Thomas, C. D., A. Cameron, R. E. Green, [and others]. 2004. Extinction risk from climate change. Nature 427:145-148.

Thomas, P. A. 2006. Mortality over 16 years of cacti in a burnt desert grassland. Plant Ecology 183:9-17.

Trader, M., M. Brooks, and J. Draper. 2006. Seed production by the non-native *Brassica tournefourtii* (Sahara mustard) along desert roadsides. Madroño 53:313-320.

Vásquez-León, M., C. T. West, and T. J. Finan. 2003. A comparative assessment of climate vulnerability: agriculture and ranching on both sides of the US-Mexico border. Global Environmental Change 13:159-173.

Van Devender, T. R. and M. A. Dimmitt. 2006. Final report on conservation of Arizona upland Sonoran Desert habitat: Status and threats of buffelgrass (*Pennisetum ciliare*) in Arizona and Sonora. Arizona-Sonora Desert Museum, Tucson, AZ.

Walsberg, G. E. 1993. Thermal consequences of diurnal microhabitat selection in a small bird. Ornis Scandinavica 24:174-182.

Weiss, J. L. and J. T. Overpeck. 2005. Is the Sonoran Desert losing its cool? Global Change Biology 11:2065-2077.

Westerling, A. L., H. G. Hidalgo, D. R. Cayan, and T. W. Swetnam. 2006. Warming and earlier spring increase western U.S. forest wildfire activity. Science 313:940-943.

Wilcove, D. S. and L. L. Master. 2005. How many endangered species are there in the United States? Frontiers in Ecology and the Environment 3:414-420.

Williams, D. G. and Z. Baruch. 2000. African grass invasion in the Americas: ecosystem consequences and the role of ecophysiology. Biological Invasions 2:213-140.

Appendix A: Species Accounts

Couch's Spadefoot
(*Scaphiopus couchii*)

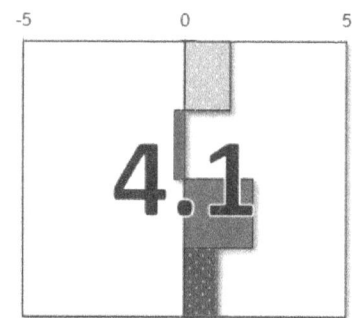

SUMMARY

The reliance of Couch's spadefoot on rainfall for suitable foraging and breeding conditions makes this species particularly vulnerable to future alterations of quantity or timing of rainfall. Conversely, this species is well adapted to fluctuating resources, thus vulnerability is reduced relative to many desert amphibians. Protection of playas and management of corridors during explosive breeding events will benefit this species.

VULNERABILITY	Score	Uncertainty
Habitat	**1.4**	14%
Physiology	**-0.3**	0%
Phenology	**2.1**	0%
Interactions	**1.0**	20%
Overall	**4.1**	**9%**

Figure Key

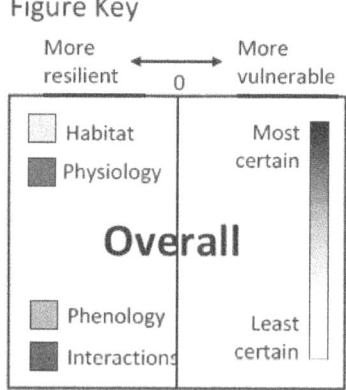

Introduction

Couch's spadefoot is not particularly rare nor is it endemic to the Sonoran desert, but spadefoots are closely tied to ephemeral rainfall patterns and, thus, are also closely tied to climate. It is also one of the few relatively common amphibians on BMGR (Hall and others 2001). In addition, it is one of the ephemeral water-breeding amphibians identified as a conservation element in the proposed biodiversity management framework for BMGR (Hall and others 2001).

BMGR-East Climate and Projections

- Annual increase in temperature 2.2 °C (4 °F) by 2050 (www.climatewizard.org, A2 emissions, ensembled GCM) and greater evaporation
- No change in average rainfall by 2050 (www.climatewizard.org, A2 emissions, ensembled GCM)
- Sonoran Desert expands northward and eastward and contracts in the southeast (Weiss and Overpeck 2005)
- More droughts and intense storms (Seager and others 2007)
- Earlier and more intense flooding (Garfin and Lenart 2007; Seager and others 2007)
- Summer monsoon changes unknown (Mitchell and others 2002)
- Grasses favored over shrubs (Esser 1992)
- Increases in invasive grasses and fires (Esser 1992; Williams and Baruch 2000)

A detailed review of projections is in the "Projections of Climate, Disturbance, and Biotic Communities" section of the main document.

Other Threats and Interactions With Climate

Couch's spadefoot is fairly common in southern Arizona but faces a number of threats, including habitat degradation. Although these threats are perhaps fewer than those faced by amphibians that are more aquatic, populations of this and similar species are also poorly studied because of their limited surface activities. Larvae are exposed to ultraviolet radiation, pollutants, disease, and predators, but these effects are somewhat reduced in the temporary pools that are generally favored. Threats may be increased for more permanent waters such as stock tanks, but with warming temperatures, these habitats may become increasingly important.

Research Needs

A number of features of this species, such as having two larval morphs and the ability to aestivate for long periods, are thought to give this species resilience to resource variation, but information is limited. These resiliencies have not been evaluated under future climate projections and may, on more detailed analysis, be found to be insufficient to maintain populations. For example, what are the population consequences of increasing proportions of carnivorous larvae as ponds dry faster? Little is known about suitability of different types of breeding ponds, but this could be important for populations as the availability of water sources change.

Management Implications

Playas and other areas that collect rainwater and have suitable soils for aestivation will be especially critical and should be protected from potentially harmful activities such as vehicle use. With greater variability in rainfall projected, temporary management for suitable and safe corridors will also be important to this species, particularly during periods of explosive breeding. Timing changes to breeding should also be anticipated and considered when establishing timing restrictions on potentially detrimental activities.

Habitat: Couch's spadefoot (*Scaphiopus couchii*)

Trait/Quality	Question	Background Info & Explanation of Score	Points
1. Area and distribution: *breeding*	Is the area or location of the associated vegetation type used for breeding activities by this species expected to change?	Occurs in various mesquite and creosote flats, mesquite bosque, shortgrass prairie, and irrigated agricultural lands (Degenhardt and others 1996) of Sonoran and Chihuahuan deserts in Arizona (Brennan and Holycross 2006). Particularly occurs near playas (Hall and others 2001). Although grasslands may increase, Couch's spadefoot also uses desert scrub habitats and, combined, these vegetation types are expected to remain approximately the same.	0
2. Area and distribution: *non-breeding*	Is the area or location of the associated vegetation type used for non-breeding activities by this species expected to change?	Same as above.	0
3. Habitat components: *breeding*	Are specific habitat components required for breeding expected to change within associated vegetation type?	Requires breeding ponds (Degenhardt and others 1996), which will be less common and more ephemeral with decreased rainfall and greater evaporation. Also observed using stock ponds for breeding.	1
4. Habitat components: *non-breeding*	Are other specific habitat components required for survival during non-breeding periods expected to change within associated vegetation type?	Needs loose soil or animal burrows to aestivate (Ruibal and others 1969). Suitable soils will be unaffected by climate.	0
5. Habitat quality	Within habitats occupied, are features of the habitat associated with better reproductive success or survival expected to change?	Deeper soils associated with better survival (Ruibal and others 1969). Likely unaffected. Longer pond duration associated with better survival of larvae (Degenhardt and others 1996), and projected changes in climate are likely to lead to shorter pond duration.	1
6. Ability to colonize new areas	What is the potential for this species to disperse?	Occasional dispersal of long distances, but generally shows high site fidelity to breeding areas (Greenberg and Tanner 2005). Although capable of long distance dispersal, its infrequency may not incur resiliency and is similar to limitations incurred by sex-biased dispersal.	0
7. Migratory or transitional habitats	Does this species require additional habitats during migration that are separated from breeding and non-breeding habitats?	No additional habitats required.	0

Physiology: Couch's spadefoot (*Scaphiopus couchii*)			
Trait/Quality	**Question**	**Background Info & Explanation of Score**	**Points**
1. Physiological thresholds	Are limiting physiological conditions expected to change?	Fairly tolerant of extreme temperatures and limited rains. Nocturnal behavior may also buffer individuals from hottest temperatures. Tolerates temperatures between 15 °C and 34 °C (Wasserman 1970). Adults able to survive during high temperatures and dry conditions (Moore 1937). Negative impacts are expected from desiccation of ponds before metamorphosis is complete and reduced longevity in larvae that develop quickly (Tinsley and Tocque 1996). Ephemeral ponds are needed for breeding and are vulnerable to very hot/dry conditions that cause them to evaporate before metamorphosis (2-6 weeks) resulting in complete mortality of tadpoles (Tinsley and Tocque 1996). Although they possess specialized adaptations, adults are prone to desiccation under extreme conditions and tadpoles are prone to desiccation before completing metamorphosis. Vulnerability to desiccation is expected to increase.	1
2. Sex ratio	Is sex ratio determined by temperature?	No.	0
3. Exposure to weather-related disturbance	Are disturbance events (e.g., severe storms, fires, floods) that affect survival or reproduction expected to change?	Nocturnal when active and hibernates much of the year underground in a burrow. Seasonal torpor used, but hibernacula are buffered from ambient temperatures. Likely escapes mortality from fire in underground retreats. No disturbances known that result in mortality.	0
4. Limitations to daily activity period	Are projected temperature or precipitation regimes that influence activity period of species expected to change?	Surface activity for movements and foraging restricted to wet periods (Degenhardt and others 1996). Decreases in rain will likely put greater restrictions on when adults and juveniles can be active.	1
5. Survival during resource fluctuation	Does this species have flexible strategies to cope with variation in resources across multiple years?	This species possesses several flexible strategies. Species can hibernate 12 months or possibly more (Ruibal and others 1969). Females can lay hundreds of eggs after rains (Degenhardt and others 1996). There are two larval morphs—one is fast growing and carnivorous and the other is slow growing and omnivorous (Degenhardt and others 1996). It is thought that this is a strategy to cope with differences in pond longevity and food availability. Ephemeral pond conditions favor carnivorous larvae (Phennig 1992). More efficient in accumulating food reserves than New Mexico spadefoot (*S. multiplicata*) and needs only approximately 2 days to accumulate reserves to aestivate for 12 months (Dimmitt and Ruibal 1980b).	-1
6. Metabolic rates	What is this species metabolic rate?	Ectothermic.	-1

Phenology: Couch's spadefoot (*Scaphiopus couchii*)

Trait/Quality	Question	Background Info & Explanation of Score	Points
1. Cues	Does this species use temperature or moisture cues to initiate activities related to fecundity or survival (e.g., hibernation, migration, breeding)?	Adults may move toward the soil surface in spring in anticipation of rains (Ruibal and others 1969). Emergence triggered by low frequency vibrations associated with heavy rain and thunder rather than soil moisture (Dimmett and Ruibal 1980a). Uses rainfall as a cue, and changes in rainfall patterns are expected.	1
2. Breeding timing	Are activities related to species' fecundity or survival tied to discrete resource peaks (e.g., food, breeding sites) that are expected to change?	Rainfall patterns will likely be altered and rainfall is required for breeding and foraging.	1
3. Mismatch potential	What is the separation in time or space between cues that initiate activities related to survival or fecundity and discrete events that provide critical resources?	Cues (rainfall/vibrations) are directly related to resource availability (ponds and termites).	-1
4. Resilience to timing mismatches during breeding	Is reproduction in this species more likely to co-occur with important events?	One breeding event per year.	1

Biotic Interactions: Couch's spadefoot (*Scaphiopus couchii*)

Trait/Quality	Question	Background Info & Explanation of Score	Points
1. Food resources	Are important food resources for this species expected to change?	Opportunistic feeding on small invertebrates including termites, ants, and crickets. Termites were a large percentage of the diet for this species in Arizona and also emerge during summer rains (Dimmitt and Ruibal 1980b). Reduced rainfall will also affect emergence of termites. Larvae are omnivorous and feed on detritus and microorganisms (Bragg 1964).	1
2. Predators	Are important predator populations expected to change?	Larvae fed on by various beetles, birds, reptiles, and mammals. Adults secrete noxious compounds from the skin (Degenhardt and others 1996). No likely alterations to overall predation rates with changing climate.	0
3. Symbionts	Are populations of symbiotic species expected to change?	No symbionts.	0

Biotic Interactions: Couch's spadefoot (*Scaphiopus couchii*)			
Trait/Quality	**Question**	**Background Info & Explanation of Score**	**Points**
4. Disease	Is prevalence of diseases known to cause widespread mortality or reproductive failure in this species expected to change?	No known diseases that result in widespread mortality.	0
5. Competitors	Are populations of important competing species expected to change?	May compete with various other temporary pond breeders, but it is thought that community structure is determined by competitive interactions that are primarily within species (Dayton and Fitzgerald 2001).	0

Literature Cited

Arizona Game and Fish Department. 2006. DRAFT. Arizona's comprehensive wildlife conservation strategy: 2005-2015. Arizona Game and Fish Department, Phoenix, Arizona.

Bagne, K. E., M. M. Friggens, and D. M. Finch. 2011. A system for assessing vulnerability of species (SAVS) to climate change. USDA Forest Service, Rocky Mountain Research Station, Gen. Tech. Rep. RMRS-GTR-257.

Bragg, A. N. 1964. Further study of predation and cannibalism in spadefoot tadpoles. Herpetologica 20:17-24.

Dayton, G. H. and L. A. Fitzgerald. 2001. Competition, predation, and the distribution of four desert anurans. Oecologia 129:430-435.

Degenhardt, W. G., C. W. Painter, and A. H. Price. 1996. Amphibians and Reptiles of New Mexico. University of New Mexico Press, Albuquerque, NM. 431 p.

Dimmitt, M. A. and R. Ruibal. 1980a. Environmental correlates of emergence in spadefoot toads (*Scaphiopus*). Journal of Herpetology 14:21-29.

Dimmitt, M. A. and R. Ruibal. 1980b. Exploitation of food resources by spadefoot toads (*Scaphiopus*). Copeia 1980:854-862.

Dukes J. S. and H.A. Mooney. 1999. Does global change increase the success of biological invaders? Trends in Ecology and Evolution 14:135-139.

Esser, Gerd. 1992. Implications of climate change for production and decomposition in grasslands and coniferous forests. Ecological Applications 2:47-54.

Garfin, G. and M. Lenart. 2007. Climate change effects on Southwest water resources. Southwest Hydrology 6:16-17.

Greenberg, C. and G. Tanner. 2005. Spatial and temporal ecology of eastern spadefoot toads on a Florida landscape. Herpetologica 61:20-28.

Hall, J. A., P. Comer, A. Gondor, R. Marshall, and S. Weinstein. 2001. Conservation Elements of and a Biodiversity Management Framework for the Barry M. Goldwater Range, Arizona. The Nature Conservancy of Arizona, Tucson.

Mitchell, D. L., D. Ivanova, R. Rabin, K. Redmond, and T. J. Brown. 2002. Gulf of California sea surface temperatures and the North American monsoon: Mechanistic implications from observations. Journal of Climate 15:2261-2281.

Moore, G. A. 1937. The spadefoot toad under drought conditions. Copeia 4:225-226.

NatureServe. 2009. NatureServe Explorer: an online encyclopedia of life [web application]. Version 7.1. NatureServe, Arlington, Virginia. Online at: http://www.natureserve.org/explorer. (Accessed: November 18, 2009)

Phennig, D. W. 1992. Polyphenism in spadefoot toad tadpoles as a logically adjusted evolutionarily stable strategy. Evolution 46:1408-1420.

Ruibal, R., L. Tevis, Jr., and V. Roig. 1969. The terrestrial ecology of the spadefoot toad *Scaphiopus hammondii*. Copeia 3:571-584.

Seager, R. T. Ming, I. Held, [and others]. 2007. Model projections of an imminent transition to a more arid climate in southwestern North America. Science 316:1181-1184.

Tinsley, R. C. and K. Tocque. 1996. The population dynamics of a desert anuran, *Scaphiopus couchii*. Austral Ecology 20:376-384.

Wasserman, A. O. 1970. *Scaphiopus couchii* baird. Catalogue of American Amphibians and Reptiles 85.1-85.4.

Weiss, J. L. and J. T. Overpeck. 2005. Is the Sonoran Desert losing its cool? Global Change Biology 11:2065-2077.

Williams, D. G. and Z. Baruch. 2000. African grass invasion in the Americas: ecosystem consequences and the role of ecophysiology. Biological Invasions 2:213-140.

Morafkai's Desert Tortoise
(*Gopherus morafkai*)

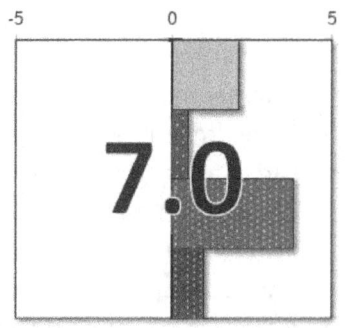

SUMMARY

Desert tortoise possesses a number of adaptations to survive in the hot and dry conditions that will likely increase with climate change. Overall, the species is expected to experience an increase in vulnerability with climate change and aspects of its biology related to phenology, primarily timing of rainfall, were identified as particularly vulnerable to detrimental changes. Although some physiological traits will likely help it cope with fluctuating resources, temperature-dependent sex ratios are vulnerable to changes from increasing temperatures. Thus, ultimate changes in populations will be partly dependent on the relative influence of physiological versus phenological traits. Adult tortoises are well adapted to survive resource fluctuations making them resilient to climate change, but the young are more vulnerable and reproduction is likely to be reduced, resulting in population changes that could take decades to be evident. Management related to succulents, fire, and water sources will be important.

VULNERABILITY	Score	Uncertainty
Habitat	**2.1**	0%
Physiology	**0.5**	17%
Phenology	**3.8**	25%
Interactions	**1.0**	40%
Overall	**7.0**	**18%**

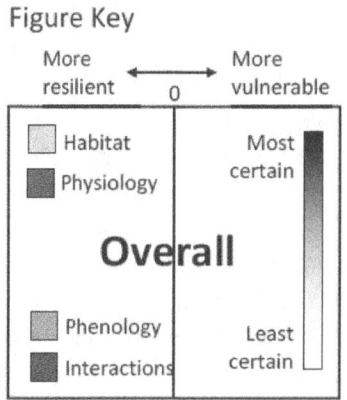

Figure Key

Introduction

This species, found in Arizona and Sinaloa and Sonora, Mexico, was recently identified as distinct from those populations found west of the Colorado River (*Gopherus agassizii*) (Murphy and others 2011). This confirms previous genetic evidence of evolutionarily separate species (Lamb and Lydeard 1994). The USFWS listed the Beaver Dam Slope population of desert tortoise in Utah as threatened in 1980 (USFWS 2008). Populations in California, Nevada, Utah, and northern Arizona (i.e., Mojave) were listed as Federally threatened in 1990. Sonoran populations are also considered threatened outside their normal range based on similarity of appearance. USFWS confirmed there is evidence that the Sonoran population is distinct and may warrant Federal listing (Federal Register, 28 August 2009, Volume 74, Number 166) but to date has not ruled on these populations or populations of the new species, which is not entirely restricted to the Sonoran Desert. Critical habitat and recovery plans were only available for the Mojave population (i.e., Agassizi's desert tortoise) at the time of this report. Monitoring data is limited for Sonoran populations, compromising estimation of population trends for Morafkai's desert tortoise.

BMGR-East Climate Projections
- Annual increase in temperature 2.2 °C (4 °F) by 2050 (www.climatewizard.org, A2 emissions, ensembled GCM) and greater evaporation

- No change in average rainfall by 2050 (www.climatewizard.org, A2 emissions, ensembled GCM)
- Summer monsoon changes unknown (Mitchell and others 2002)
- More droughts and intense storms (Seager and others 2007)
- Earlier and more intense flooding (Garfin and Lenart 2007; Seager and others 2007)
- Grasses favored over shrubs (Esser 1992)
- Increases in invasive grasses and fires (Esser 1992; Williams and Baruch 2000)
- CAM plants (succulents and cacti) will be resilient to increasing temperatures
- A detailed review of projections is in the "Projections of Climate, Disturbance, and Biotic Communities" section of the main text
- Other Threats and Interactions with Climate

Numerous threats have been identified previously, including loss and degradation of habitat, collection for the pet trade, disease, predation, and increased drought associated with climate change (USFWS 2008). Increases in ravens in urban areas may increase predation of hatchling tortoises in surrounding natural habitats (Kristan and Boarman 2001). Release of pet tortoises into the wild may also spread disease (USFWS 2008). Off-road vehicle use threatens burrows and can also result in the crushing of individuals. Competition with livestock and other herbivores for food is a concern. Environmental toxins have been suggested to play a role in disease susceptibility (Boarman 2002). None of these is likely to interact with changes in climate except indirectly through socioeconomic changes that affect regional demographics.

The spread of non-native grasses increases fire frequency and may reduce native plants and habitat quality. Increases in fire and temperatures are predicted to occur with climate change, exacerbating this problem. Development of lands for alternative energy production is likely and may affect tortoise habitats adjacent to BMGR. Wind development may be compatible with desert tortoise habitat (Lovich and Daniels 2000), but there are concerns about habitat loss from solar developments (USFWS 2008).

Research Needs
Research on Sonoran populations of desert tortoise was assumed to be on Morafkai's desert tortoise. USFWS (2008) identified a number of areas for further research on desert tortoises, including characterization of stable age distributions for increasing populations, determination of factors that influence the distribution of desert tortoises, habitat restoration, improvements for population and mitigation models, desert tortoise diseases and their effects, and resolving population structure of the desert tortoise across its range.

In relation to climate change, research on distribution and habitat use relative to projected vegetation changes will be particularly important. This type of analysis could also include detailed projections related to soil surface temperature and moisture and breeding distribution to evaluate the potential for issues related to temperature-dependent sex ratios and hatching success. Although tortoises can survive long periods without water, its availability during critical periods may help mitigate detrimental effects of summer drought. Research related to the potential for water developments or other habitat modifications to improve tortoise habitats would be valuable. Research is also lacking on the interaction of tortoise diseases and climate variables as well as frequency of disease mortality in populations outside the Mojave Desert, California.

Management Implications
Detrimental effects of climate change were projected to have a greater impact on young tortoises than adults, thus changes in adult populations would not be expected for many years and reproductive success should be consider as part of any monitoring program. Thermal environment is key, thus management that maintains vegetative cover and reduces soil compaction that prevents burrowing is important (Zimmerman 1994). In addition, management that maintains the thermal environment will become more critical as temperatures

increase and rainfall levels become more variable. In creating protected areas for desert tortoise, the thermal aspects of these areas, such as slope or shade, should be considered to ensure the continued benefits of these locations as temperatures rise. Management related to enhancement of temporary rainfall catchment may also be beneficial.

Major vulnerabilities for this species involved timing because important reproductive variables such as breeding and incubation times as well as sex ratio are temperature and/or rainfall related. Thus, timing of important activities will likely be altered in this species, but the outcome of such changes is unknown. The outcome will depend on complex interactions, microhabitats occupied, annual variability, and how closely timing in tortoise activities adjusts with timing in vegetation growth or other important events. For this assessment, we assumed timing changes increased the likelihood of detrimental impacts relative to current conditions, but we recognize that tortoises may prove resilient to some degree. Management that includes a large range and various microhabitats will likely enhance resilience to timing issues.

Although not currently a major threat at BMGR, fire and its interaction with introduced plants can significantly alter vegetation and may be an emerging issue that warrants monitoring. Succulents are prone to fire mortality, and fires are expected to increase with climate change and invasive plants, some of which increase fire occurrence, may be well adapted to changing climate conditions (Dukes and Mooney 1999). At the same time, invasive grasses and forbs appear to provide suitable forage for desert tortoises, thus increases in invasives may be beneficial to some extent although the concentration of these plants along roadsides adds to tortoise mortality risk. BMGR already actively controls some invasive plants, such as tumbleweeds, and fire risk should be evaluated for critical tortoise habitats such as those dominated by palo verde and cacti or that have favorable thermal conditions.

HABITAT: Morafkai's desert tortoise (*Gopherus morafkai*)			
Trait/Quality	**Question**	**Background Info & Explanation of Score**	**Points**
1. Area and distribution: *breeding*	Is the area or location of the associated vegetation type used for breeding activities by this species expected to change?	Use a variety of desert vegetation types, including scrub communities associated with cacti and palo verde. Southwestern Arizona is near the center of the range for desert tortoise, which extends from Utah into Mexico. Vegetation associations include creosote bush, palo verde-mixed cacti, and saguaro-ocotillo cacti associations. Native plants of these vegetation types are not likely to be reduced by increasing temperatures (up to year 2050). Increased fire occurrence is projected but will depend on ground cover. Sonoran desert habitats may expand to the north, but these regions will be more prone to increased fire frequency because of higher rainfall levels and already high levels of invasive grasses.	0
2. Area and distribution: *non-breeding*	Is the area or location of the associated vegetation type used for non-breeding activities by this species expected to change?	Same as above.	0
3. Habitat components: *breeding*	Are specific habitat components required for breeding expected to change within associated vegetation type?	Suitable burrows and soils are required for breeding. Not expected to change.	0
4. Habitat components: *non-breeding*	Are other specific habitat components required for survival during non-breeding periods expected to change within associated vegetation type?	Required habitat elements include periodic water sources and suitable locations for burrows. Temporary pools created by rainfall appear to be important, particularly during the summer months, for growth and survival (Nagy and others 1998). In the San Pedro Valley, Arizona, desert tortoises hibernated in burrows excavated in friable soils on steep, south-facing slopes, probably for thermal advantage (Bailey and others 1995). Generally dig deep burrows, but some Sonoran tortoises aestivate in rock crevices or under boulders (De Vos and others 1983; NatureServe 2009). Need suitable areas for burrows (washes, crevices, and friable soils). Burrows are not likely to be affected by climate, but periodic water sources will be reduced with warmer temperatures and more variable rainfall.	1
5. Habitat quality	Within habitats occupied, are features of the habitat associated with better reproductive success or survival expected to change?	Greater spring annual production may be associated with a greater proportion of females breeding and greater reproductive success. Winter precipitation, which correlates with spring annual production, is expected to remain similar to current levels, but greater variability is anticipated along with greater evaporation. Projections for summer precipitation are more uncertain. Greater vegetative cover, particularly shrubs, may increase survival through improving the thermal environment. Increasing fires will likely reduce native desert shrubs in some areas and many shrubs are drought deciduous.	1

HABITAT: Morafkai's desert tortoise (*Gopherus morafkai*)			
Trait/Quality	**Question**	**Background Info & Explanation of Score**	**Points**
6. Ability to colonize new areas	What is the potential for this species to disperse?	Desert tortoises are not territorial and generally occupy home ranges of fewer than 50 ha, though individuals may move several kilometers (NatureServe 2009). Males may also have larger home ranges than females. Can move several kilometers, but movements are generally limited and are often blocked by roads and fences. Probably limited in their ability to expand into new habitats within limited time periods.	1
7. Migratory or transitional habitats	Does this species require additional habitats during migration that are separated from breeding and non-breeding habitats?	Do not migrate through or require transitional habitats.	0

Physiology: Morafkai's desert tortoise (*Gopherus morafkai*)			
Trait/Quality	**Question**	**Background Info & Explanation of Score**	**Points**
1. Physiological thresholds	Are limiting physiological conditions expected to change?	Adults are effective at retaining water and store it in the bladder for up to a year (Peterson 1996; Henen and others 1998). Adults are capable of withstanding large imbalances in electrolytes and water (Henen 1997). In addition, they can switch from producing urea to more water-conserving uric acid (NatureServe 2009). Young tortoises are more prone to dehydration and starvation than larger adults (NatureServe 2009). Eggs are laid in shallow depressions generally near the entrance of the burrow. For Mojave tortoises, incubation temperatures need to be between 26 °C and 33 °C but could be successful at up to 35 °C. Soil moisture above 4% can compromise hatching (Spotila and others 1994). Lower survival rates in the Mojave Desert were associated with droughts (Longshore and others 2003). Distribution is thought to be limited by aridity in the lower Colorado River Valley (Van Devender 2002) and by wet climates in the tropics that promote fungus pathogens (Bury and others 2002). Droughts, which are expected to increase, are associated with higher mortality, particularly for juveniles.	1
2. Sex ratio	Is sex ratio determined by temperature?	Tortoises have temperature-determined sex ratios, with males hatching at lower temperatures and females at higher temperatures. In Nevada, the pivotal temperature for determining sex was found to be 31.8 °C (Spotila and others 1994).	1
3. Exposure to weather-related disturbance	Are disturbance events (e.g., severe storms, fires, floods) that affect survival or reproduction expected to change?	Hibernacula of females were in shorter burrows than males and thus subject to greater temperature fluctuations (Bailey and others 1995). Male hibernacula may be more buffered from extreme conditions than female hibernacula. Burrow excavation behaviors may be flexible and individuals probably can adjust burrow dimensions to adequately buffer from ambient temperatures. Slow moving, thus may be prone to direct	0

Physiology: Morafkai's desert tortoise (*Gopherus morafkai*)

Trait/Quality	Question	Background Info & Explanation of Score	Points
		mortality during fires, but fire risk in these habitats is generally not high. No known mortality associated with flooding or fires.	
4. Limitations to daily activity period	Are projected temperature or precipitation regimes that influence activity period of species expected to change?	Spend much of the year inactive although activity is strongly associated with temperature. Active periods and movements were reduced during a drought year as compared to a wet year in the Mojave Desert, which may be an adaptation to save energy when resources are limited (Duda 1999). Desert tortoises also tended to be inactive during hot temperatures such as mid-day in summer and more active following summer rains (Zimmerman 1994; Duda 1999). Activity patterns and burrow use are sensitive to surface temperatures (Zimmerman 1994). During summer, tortoises generally sleep under bushes at night and activities are still primarily diurnal, although more limited during hot temperatures (Zimmerman 1994). Activity periods likely reduced with higher temperatures and greater evaporation.	1
5. Survival during resource fluctuation	Does this species have flexible strategies to cope with variation in resources across multiple years?	Desert tortoises can store water in the bladder and switch between production of urea and uric acid. Females can also store sperm and sperm can be stored from the previous year (Rostal and others 1994). Agassizi's desert tortoises have also been known to construct rainwater catchments (Medica and others 1980). These strategies may be helpful as resources and populations fluctuate across years.	-1
6. Metabolic rates	What is this species metabolic rate?	Desert tortoises have low metabolic rates as compared to other reptiles and can tolerate long drought periods (Peterson 1996).	-1

Phenology: Morafkai's desert tortoise (*Gopherus morafkai*)

Trait/Quality	Question	Background Info & Explanation of Score	Points
1. Cues	Does this species use temperature or moisture cues to initiate activities related to fecundity or survival (e.g., hibernation, migration, breeding)?	Temperature and moisture related to emergence from hibernacula, after which mating and egg laying occur. Emergence from hibernacula varies with temperature and rainfall, and individuals may emerge opportunistically (NatureServe 2009). Desert tortoises hibernate in winter and may also aestivate during hot summer temperatures. Tortoises will emerge periodically from burrows during winter to bask or move between burrows (Averill-Murray 2000).	1
2. Breeding timing	Are activities related to species' fecundity or survival tied to discrete resource peaks (e.g., food, breeding sites) that are expected to change?	Rainfall is important to digestion and growth. Quantity and timing of rainfall was found to be an important interaction responsible for variation. Timing and quantity of rainfall will likely be altered with climate change. Incubation time varies with temperature. Differences in female hibernacula may influence individual timing of emergence (Bailey and others 1995).	1

USDA Forest Service RMRS-GTR-284. 2012.

Phenology: Morafkai's desert tortoise (*Gopherus morafkai*)			
Trait/Quality	**Question**	**Background Info & Explanation of Score**	**Points**
3. Mismatch potential	What is the separation in time or space between cues that initiate activities related to survival or fecundity and discrete events that provide critical resources?	Spermatogenesis and mating occurs in the fall. Mating also occurs in spring, after emergence from hibernation, from March to April (Rostal and others 1994). Eggs incubate >85 days following fertilization and egg laying in the spring. Because hibernation emergence is likely cued by temperature, it is not distant from conditions that will affect resources.	0
4. Resilience to timing mismatches during breeding	Is reproduction in this species more likely to co-occur with important events?	Egg laying occurs from May to early July, and in some regions, females can have a second clutch, although Sonoran populations seem to have a single clutch per year (NatureServe 2009). Proportion of females reproducing in a given year appears to be related to winter and spring rainfall (Averill-Murray 2000). Breed once per year (or less) in the spring.	1

Biotic Interactions: Morafkai's desert tortoise (*Gopherus morafkai*)			
Trait/Quality	**Question**	**Background Info & Explanation of Score**	**Points**
1. Food resources	Are important food resources for this species expected to change?	Eat a variety of plant species. Herbaceous growth will fluctuate with rainfall and likely become more variable. Grasses may increase with higher temperatures and increased fires, but forbs are higher quality forage than grasses. Although there will be some years of high herbaceous growth, increasing droughts and higher temperatures will likely reduce vegetation available in many years. Desert tortoises feed primarily on vegetation but also some insects (NatureServe 2009). Annual grasses eaten include non-native species such as red brome (*Bromus rubens*). Forbs, both native and non-native, were processed more efficiently, required less water to digest, and contained more nitrogen than grasses (Nagy and others 1998). Dry forage along with consumption of rain water is important to building energy stores (Peterson 1996).	1
2. Predators	Are important predator populations expected to change?	Predation at nests may be high (Germano 1994). A large range of predators eat hatchlings and juveniles (USFWS 2008). Increased urban development has been implicated in increasing ravens and thus tortoise predation (Kristan and Boarman 2001), but this interaction may not be present in Sonoran populations (Averill-Murray 2000). Predation of eggs is fairly high but opportunistic by a wide variety of predators. No current urban development near BMGR-East that is likely to significantly increase raven populations on DoD lands in the near future.	0
3. Symbionts	Are populations of symbiotic species expected to change?	No symbionts. Winter burrows may be used communally, but not known how common this behavior is, although it is assumed it decreases energy needed for thermoregulation.	0

Biotic Interactions: Morafkai's desert tortoise (*Gopherus morafkai*)			
Trait/Quality	Question	Background Info & Explanation of Score	Points
4. Disease	Is prevalence of diseases known to cause widespread mortality or reproductive failure in this species expected to change?	At least two diseases have been implicated in widespread mortality: upper respiratory tract disease caused by mycoplasma (Jacobson and others 1991) and cutaneous dyskeratosis or shell disease (Jacobson and others 1994). Most disease-related declines have been documented for Mojave populations and there have been no recent declines attributed to disease in Sonoran populations (Averill-Murray 2000). The majority of Sonoran tortoises from one study, however, were recorded as having shell disease, though it was not implicated in mortality (Averill-Murray 2000). Transmission may be increased by release of captive-reared or pet tortoises, or possibly ravens. Disease susceptibility has also been linked to toxins such as arsenic. Susceptible to disease, though most mortality has been documented in Mojave populations. No known relationship between virulence or transmission of these diseases and climate.	0
5. Competitors	Are populations of important competing species expected to change?	Competition for forage is thought to occur with livestock and other herbivores (USFWS 2008).BMGR does not have livestock grazing. Changes in climate would be most likely to decrease competing native grazers, but populations of potential competitive species are low.	0

Literature Cited

Arizona Game and Fish Department. 2006. DRAFT. Arizona's comprehensive wildlife conservation strategy: 2005-2015. Arizona Game and Fish Department, Phoenix, Arizona.

Averill-Murray, R.C., and C.M. Klug. 2000. Monitoring and ecology of Sonoran desert tortoises in Arizona. Nongame and Endangered Wildlife Program Technical Report 161. Arizona Game and Fish Department, Phoenix, Arizona.

Bagne, K. E., M. M. Friggens, and D. M. Finch. 2011. A system for assessing vulnerability of species (SAVS) to climate change. USDA Forest Service, Rocky Mountain Research Station, Gen. Tech. Rep. RMRS-GTR-257.

Bailey, S. J., C. R. Schwalbe, and C. H. Lowe. 1995. Hibernaculum Use by a Population of Desert Tortoises (*Gopherus agassizii*) in the Sonoran Desert. Journal of Herpetology 29:361-369.

Boarman, W. I. 2002. Threats to desert tortoise populations: a critical review of the literature. U.S. Geological Survey, Western Ecological Research Center, Sacramento, California.

Bury, R. B., D. J. Germano, T. R. Van Devender, and B. E. Martin. 2002. Chapter 5: the Desert Tortoise in Mexico. Pages 86-108 In T. R. Van Devender, ed., The Sonoran Desert Tortoise: Natural History, Biology, and Conservation.

Cox, J. R. and G. B. Ruhle. 1986. Influence of climatic and edaphic factors on the distribution of *Eragrostis lehmanniana* nees in Arizona, USA. African Journal of Range and Forage Science: 3.

Duda, J. J., A. J. Krzysik, and J. E. Freilich. 1999. Effects of drought on desert tortoise movement and activity. The Journal of Wildlife Management 63:1181-1192.

Dukes, J. S. and H. A. Mooney. 1999. Does global change increase the success of biological invaders? Trends in Ecology and Evolution 14:135-139.

Ehleringer, J. R., S. L. Phillips, W. S. F. Schuster, and D. R. Sandqui. 1991. Differential utilization of summer rains by desert plants. Oecologia 88:430-434.

Esser, Gerd. 1992. Implications of climate change for production and decomposition in grasslands and coniferous forests. Ecological Applications 2:47-54.

Garfin, G. and M. Lenart. 2007. Climate change effects on Southwest water resources. Southwest Hydrology 6:16-17.

Germano, D. J. 1994. Growth and age at maturity of North American tortoises in relation to regional climates. Canadian Journal of Zoology 72:918-931.

Henen, B. T. 1997. Seasonal and annual energy budgets of female desert tortoises (*Gopherus agassizii*). Ecology 78:283-296.

Henen, B. T., C. C. Peterson, I. R. Wallis, K. H. Berry, and K. A. Nagy. 1998. Effects of climatic variation on field metabolism and water relations of desert tortoises. Oecologia 117:365-373.

Hoffmeister, D. F. 1986. Mammals of Arizona. University of Arizona Press and Arizona Game and Fish Dept. 602 p.

Jacobson, E. R., J. M. Gaskin, M. B. Brown, R. K. Harris, C. H. Gardiner, J. L. LaPointe, H. P. Adams, and C. Reggiardo. 1991. Chronic upper respiratory tract disease of free-ranging desert tortoises (*Xerobates agassizii*). Journal of Wildlife Diseases 27:296-316.

Jacobson, E. R., T. J. Wronski, J. Schumacher, C. Reggiardo, and K. H. Berry. 1994. Cutaneous dyskeratosis in free-ranging desert tortoises, *Gopherus agassizii*, in the Colorado Desert of Southern California. Journal of Zoo and Wildlife Medicine 25:68-81.

Kristan, W. B. and W. I. Boarman. 2003. Spatial pattern of risk of common raven predation on desert tortoises. Ecology 84:2432-2443.

Longshore, K. M., J. R. Jaeger, and J. M. Sappington. 2003. Desert tortoise (*Gopherus agassizii*) survival at two eastern Mojave Desert sites: death by short-term drought? Journal of Herpetology 37:169-177.

Lovich, J. E., and R. Daniels. 2000. Environmental characteristics of desert tortoise (*Gopherus agassizii*) burrow locations in an altered industrial landscape. Chelonian Conservation and Biology 3:714-721.

Medica, P. A., R. B. Bury, and R. A. Luckenbach. 1980. Drinking and construction of water catchments by the desert tortoise, *Gopherus agassizii*, in the Mojave Desert. Herpetologica 36:301-304.

McLaughlin, S. E. and J. P. Bowers. 1982. Effects of wildfire on a Sonoran Desert plant community. Ecology 63:246-248.

Mitchell, D. L., D. Ivanova, R. Rabin, K. Redmond, and T. J. Brown. 2002. Gulf of California sea surface temperatures and the North American monsoon: mechanistic implications from observations. Journal of Climate 15:2261-2281.

Murphy, R. W., K. H. Berry, T. Edwards, A. E. Leviton, A. Lathrop, and J. D. Riedle. 2011. The dazed and confused identity of Agassiz's land tortoise, *Gopherus agassizii* (Testudines, Testudinidae) with the description of a new species, and its consequences for conservation. ZooKeys 113: 39-71. doi:10.3897/zookeys.113.1353.

Nagy, K. A., B. T. Henen, and D. B. Vyas. 1998. Nutritional quality of native and introduced food plants of wild desert tortoises. Journal of Herpetology 32:260-267.

NatureServe. 2009. NatureServe Explorer: an online encyclopedia of life [web application]. Version 7.1. NatureServe, Arlington, Virginia. Online at: http://www.natureserve.org/explorer. (Accessed: November 18, 2009)

Peterson, C. C. 1996. Ecological energetics of the desert tortoise (*Gopherus agassizii*): effects of rainfall and drought. Ecology 77:1831-1844.

Pinkava, D. J. 1999. Cactaceae cactus family, part three Cylindropuntia. Journal of the Arizona-Nevada Academy of Science 32(1):32-47.

Rostal, D. C., V. A. Lance, J. S. Grumbles, and A. C. Alberts. 1994. Seasonal reproductive cycle of the desert tortoise (*Gopherus agassizii*) in the eastern Mojave Desert. Herpetological Monographs 8:72-82.

Seager, R., T. Ming, I. Held, [and others]. 2007. Model projections of an imminent transition to a more arid climate in southwestern North America. Science 316:1181-1184.

Smith, S. D., B. Didden-Zopfy, and P. S. Nobel. 1984. High-temperature responses of North American cacti. Ecology 65:643-651.

Spotila, J. R., L. C. Zimmerman, C. A. Binckley,[and others]. 1994. Effects of incubation conditions on sex determination, hatching success, and growth of hatchling desert tortoises, *Gopherus agassizii*. Herpetological Monographs 8:103-116.

U.S. Fish and Wildlife Service (USFWS). 2008. Draft revised recovery plan for the Mojave population of the desert tortoise (*Gopherus agassizii*). U.S. Fish and Wildlife Service, California and Nevada Region, Sacramento, CA. 209 p.

Van Devender, T. R. 2002. Chapter 1: Natural History of the Sonoran Tortoise in Arizona. Pages 3-28 In T. R. Van Devender, ed., The Sonoran Desert Tortoise: Natural History, Biology, and Conservation. University of Arizona Press, Tucson, AZ.

Van Devender, T. R. and M. A. Dimmitt. 2006. Final report on conservation of Arizona upland Sonoran Desert habitat: status and threats of buffelgrass (*Pennisetum ciliare*) in Arizona and Sonora. Arizona-Sonora Desert Museum, Tucson, AZ.

Weiss, J. L. and J. T. Overpeck. 2005. Is the Sonoran Desert losing its cool? Global Change Biology 11:2065-2077.

Williams, D. G. and Z. Baruch. 2000. African grass invasion in the Americas: ecosystem consequences and the role of ecophysiology. Biological Invasions 2:213-140.

Zimmerman, L. C., M. P. O'Connor, S. J. Bulova, J. R. Spotila, S. J. Kemp, and C. J. Salice. 1994. Thermal ecology of desert tortoises in the eastern Mojave Desert: seasonal patterns of operative and body temperatures, and microhabitat utilization. Herpetological Monographs 8:45-59.

Saddled Leaf-nosed Snake
(*Phyllorhynchus browni*)

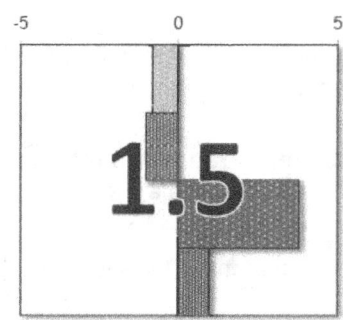

SUMMARY

The saddled leaf-nosed snake may be vulnerable to climate change because of its specialized diet of snake and lizard eggs, although overall, the predicted increase in vulnerability for this species was limited. Phenology was an area of high vulnerability for this species as the timing of hibernation and breeding may shift. Vulnerability of this species will depend on how other species respond; thus, predicting future population changes is particularly complex and uncertainty is high.

Figure Key

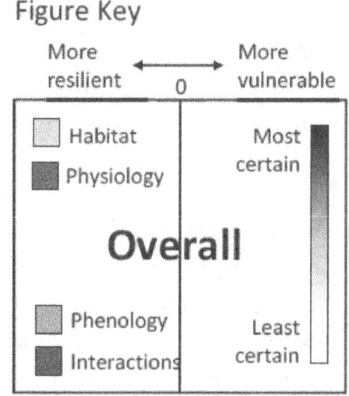

VULNERABILITY	Score	Uncertainty
Habitat	**-0.8**	29%
Physiology	**-1.0**	50%
Phenology	**3.8**	25%
Interactions	**1.0**	60%
Overall	**1.5**	**41%**

Introduction

The saddled leaf-nosed snake was formerly thought to be a subspecies of spotted leaf-nosed snake (*Phyllorhynchus decurtatus*). Little is known about populations and the species is listed as being of unknown status in the Arizona State Wildlife Action Plan (AGFD 2006). The U.S. Forest Service designates it as sensitive. The proposed biodiversity management framework for BMGR suggests that the saddled leaf-nosed snake will be vulnerable to climate change effects (Hall and others 2001).

BMGR-East Climate and Projections

- Annual increase in temperature 2.2 °C (4 °F) by 2050 (www.climatewizard.org, A2 emissions, ensembled GCM) and greater evaporation
- No change in average rainfall by 2050 (www.climatewizard.org, A2 emissions, ensembled GCM)
- Sonoran Desert expands northward and eastward, and contracts in the southeast (Weiss and Overpeck 2005)
- More droughts and intense storms (Seager and others 2007)
- Earlier and more intense flooding (Garfin and Lenart 2007; Seager and others 2007)
- Summer monsoon changes unknown (Mitchell and others 2002)
- Grasses favored over shrubs (Esser 1992)
- Increases in invasive grasses and fires (Esser 1992; Williams and Baruch 2000)

A detailed review of projections is in the "Projections of Climate, Disturbance, and Biotic Communities" section of the main text.

Other Threats and Interactions with Climate

The specialist diet of this species may increase its vulnerability to population declines with climate change (Hall and others 2001). Other snake and lizard species may be vulnerable to declines and, in turn, may affect populations of leaf-nosed snakes. Military activities that use roads at night may increase risk for this species, but climate is not expected to alter this impact. Vehicular use of dunes, including recreational and law enforcement use, could also negatively impact this species, and border patrol activities could conceivably increase. Buffering of climate impacts varies with factors such as irrigation and government programs, both of which predict that drought impacts will be less severe in the United States as compared to Mexico (Vásquez-León and others 2003). In the absence of alterations to immigration policies, increased illegal traffic at the international border is expected.

Research Needs

The saddled leaf-nosed snake is a poorly understood species, so little information is available to assess its vulnerability and almost all aspects of its natural history need more study. Its secretive nocturnal habits add to problems with research and population monitoring. The restricted diet of this snake will likely increase its vulnerability to declines, but its ability to switch to other food sources is unknown. *P. decurtatus* eats small lizards.

Management Implications

Various nighttime military training activities, particularly those that involve vehicles, may affect this species through direct mortality or disturbance. Daytime vehicle use on dunes can also impact burrows or buried snakes. Although most human threats to this species are not expected to increase with climate change, border patrol activities, and thus vehicular use, may increase with climate change if drought stress increases illegal immigration in the region. Reducing mortality sources could help maintain populations if other threats increase. Travel through leaf-nosed snake habitats should be managed to reduce impacts. Protection of other snake and lizard species will ensure adequate food resources for this species.

USDA Forest Service RMRS-GTR-284. 2012.

Habitat: Saddled leaf-nosed snake (*Phyllorhynchus browni*)

Trait/Quality	Question	Background Info & Explanation of Score	Points
1. Area and distribution: *breeding*	Is the area or location of the associated vegetation type used for breeding activities by this species expected to change?	In the northern part of its range, this snake inhabits desertscrub with mesquite, saltbush, creosote bush, palo verde, and saguaro cactus. In southern areas, it frequents thornscrub and the lower edge of thornforest (Stebbins, 1985). Usually occurs in foothills (Brennan and Holycross 2006). No expected change in area occupied by this vegetation type on BMGR.	0
2. Area and distribution: *non-breeding*	Is the area or location of the associated vegetation type used for non-breeding activities by this species expected to change?	Same as above.	0
3. Habitat components: *breeding*	Are specific habitat components required for breeding expected to change within associated vegetation type?	Lays eggs underground in burrow. No expected changes in suitable soils for burrowing.	0
4. Habitat components: *non-breeding*	Are other specific habitat components required for survival during non-breeding periods expected to change within associated vegetation type?	Uses burrows for hibernation and digs its own burrow. No expected changes in suitable soils for burrowing.	0
5. Habitat quality	Within habitats occupied, are features of the habitat associated with better reproductive success or survival expected to change?	None known.	0
6. Ability to colonize new areas	What is the potential for this species to disperse?	Unknown dispersal, but assumed to be mobile without major barriers.	-1
7. Migratory or transitional habitats	Does this species require additional habitats during migration that are separated from breeding and non-breeding habitats?	Not migratory.	0

Physiology: Saddled leaf-nosed snake (*Phyllorhynchus browni*)

Trait/Quality	Question	Background Info & Explanation of Score	Points
1. Physiological thresholds	Are limiting physiological conditions expected to change?	Little information. Range is Arizona and Mexico (Brennan and Holycross 2006). Not expected to exceed critical temperatures in habitats occupied, and not generally exposed to the hottest temperatures.	0
2. Sex ratio	Is sex ratio determined by temperature?	No.	0
3. Exposure to weather-related disturbance	Are disturbance events (e.g., severe storms, fires, floods) that affect survival or reproduction expected to change?	Hibernates during cold months and is often buried in sand (Brennan and Holycross 2006). Likely to escape at least some disturbance events. No other information.	0
4. Limitations to daily activity period	Are projected temperature or precipitation regimes that influence activity period of species expected to change?	Wholly nocturnal, and no anticipated changes in activity periods.	0
5. Survival during resource fluctuation	Does this species have flexible strategies to cope with variation in resources across multiple years?	No flexible strategies known.	0
6. Metabolic rates	What is this species metabolic rate?	Ectothermic.	-1

Phenology: Saddled leaf-nosed snake (*Phyllorhynchus browni*)

Trait/Quality	Question	Background Info & Explanation of Score	Points
1. Cues	Does this species use temperature or moisture cues to initiate activities related to fecundity or survival (e.g., hibernation, migration, breeding)?	Temperature is likely cue for hibernation.	1
2. Breeding timing	Are activities related to species' fecundity or survival tied to discrete resource peaks (e.g., food, breeding sites) that are expected to change?	Limited information but it is assumed that eggs are laid in summer (BISON-M). Eggs are thought to be laid in June to July in *decurtatus*. Hatchlings emerge starting in July (Brennan and Holycross 2006). Resource peaks are not known, although may time breeding to availability of eggs of other snakes, which will be subject to phenological changes in breeding.	1
3. Mismatch potential	What is the separation in time or space between cues that initiate activities related to survival or fecundity and discrete events that provide critical resources?	Cues not expected to be distant from activities such as breeding.	0

Phenology: Saddled leaf-nosed snake (*Phyllorhynchus browni*)			
Trait/Quality	**Question**	**Background Info & Explanation of Score**	**Points**
4. Resilience to timing mismatches during breeding	Is reproduction in this species more likely to co-occur with important events?	One reproductive event per year.	1

Biotic Interactions: Saddled leaf-nosed snake (*Phyllorhynchus browni*)			
Trait/Quality	**Question**	**Background Info & Explanation of Score**	**Points**
1. Food resources	Are important food resources for this species expected to change?	This species is a specialist that mostly eats eggs of snakes and lizards (Stebbins 1985, Brennan and Holycross 2006). Although various lizards and snakes may be resilient to climate change, reproduction is more sensitive and likely reduced in many species by increasing droughts.	1
2. Predators	Are important predator populations expected to change?	Not known, but assumed to have various predators. Not expected to change overall.	0
3. Symbionts	Are populations of symbiotic species expected to change?	None.	0
4. Disease	Is prevalence of diseases known to cause widespread mortality or reproductive failure in this species expected to change?	None known.	0
5. Competitors	Are populations of important competing species expected to change?	None known.	0

Literature Cited

Arizona Game and Fish Department. 2006. DRAFT. Arizona's comprehensive wildlife conservation strategy: 2005-2015. Arizona Game and Fish Department, Phoenix, AZ.

Bagne, K. E., M. M. Friggens, and D. M. Finch. 2011. A system for assessing vulnerability of species (SAVS) to climate change. USDA Forest Service, Rocky Mountain Research Station, Gen. Tech. Rep. RMRS-GTR-257.

BISON-M. Biotic Information System of New Mexico. New Mexico Game and Fish Department. Online at: http://www.bison-m.org.

Brennan, T. C. and A. T. Holycross. 2006. A field guide to amphibians and reptiles in Arizona. Arizona Game and Fish Department. Phoenix, AZ.

Esser, G. 1992. Implications of climate change for production and decomposition in grasslands and coniferous forests. Ecological Applications 2:47-54.

Garfin, G. and M. Lenart. 2007. Climate change effects on Southwest water resources. Southwest Hydrology 6:16-17.

Hall, J. A., P. Comer, A. Gondor, R. Marshall, and S. Weinstein. 2001. Conservation Elements of and a Biodiversity Management Framework for the Barry M. Goldwater Range, Arizona. The Nature Conservancy of Arizona, Tucson.

Mitchell, D. L., D. Ivanova, R. Rabin, K. Redmond, and T. J. Brown. 2002. Gulf of California sea surface temperatures and the North American monsoon: mechanistic implications from observations. Journal of Climate 15:2261-2281.

NatureServe. 2009. NatureServe Explorer: an online encyclopedia of life [web application]. Version 7.1. NatureServe, Arlington, Virginia. Online at: http://www.natureserve.org/explorer. (Accessed: November 18, 2009).

Seager, R., T. Ming, I. Held, [and others]. 2007. Model projections of an imminent transition to a more arid climate in southwestern North America. Science 316:1181-1184.

Stebbins, R. C. 1985. A Field Guide to Western Reptiles and Amphibians. Second Edition. National Audubon Society. Houghton Mifflin Co., Boston and New York.

Vásquez-León, M., C. T. West, and T. J. Finan. 2003. A comparative assessment of climate vulnerability: agriculture and ranching on both sides of the US-Mexico border. Global Environmental Change 13:159-173.

Weiss, J. L. and J. T. Overpeck. 2005. Is the Sonoran Desert losing its cool? Global Change Biology 11:2065-2077.

Williams, D. G. and Z. Baruch. 2000. African grass invasion in the Americas: ecosystem consequences and the role of ecophysiology. Biological Invasions 2:213-140.

Red-backed Whiptail
(*Aspidoscelis xanthonota*)

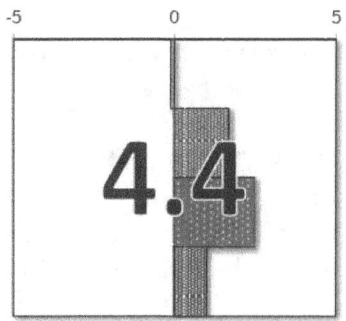

SUMMARY

Red-backed whiptails are expected to have some increased vulnerability to declines associated with future climate change. Phenology, as related to both seasonal and daily activity, is an area of vulnerability, although phenological relationships are not well known for this species. Management of xeroriparian habitats, particularly the prevention of invasion by non-native grasses, as well as protection of large trees and shrubs will be important.

VULNERABILITY	Score	Uncertainty
Habitat	**-0.1**	29%
Physiology	1.7	50%
Phenology	2.5	25%
Interactions	1.0	60%
Overall	**4.4**	**45%**

Figure Key

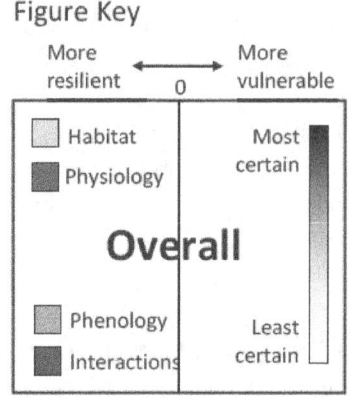

Introduction

Formerly, red-backed whiptail was a subspecies of the canyon spotted whiptail and identified as *Cneimidophorous burti xanthonotus* or *Aspidoscelis burti xanthonota*. It potentially occurs in xeroriparian scrub in the Sand Tank Mountains (Hall and others 2001). Arizona State Fish and Game identifies it as a species of greatest conservation need, Tier 1B, in the Arizona State Wildlife Action Plan (AGFD 2006). Furthermore, it was identified as potentially vulnerable to climate change effects on BMGR (Hall and others 2001). BMGR is the edge of the range for this species; thus, climate-related shifts in distribution will likely affect its abundance and occurrence locally (Hall and others 2001).

BMGR-East Climate and Projections

- Annual increase in temperature 2.2 °C (4 °F) by 2050 (www.climatewizard.org, A2 emissions, ensembled GCM) and greater evaporation
- No change in average rainfall by 2050 (www.climatewizard.org, A2 emissions, ensembled GCM)
- Sonoran Desert expands northward and eastward, and contracts in the southeast (Weiss and Overpeck 2005)
- More droughts and intense storms (Seager and others 2007)
- Earlier and more intense flooding (Garfin and Lenart 2007; Seager and others 2007)
- Summer monsoon changes unknown (Mitchell and others 2002)
- Grasses favored over shrubs (Esser 1992)
- Increases in invasive grasses and fires (Esser 1992; Williams and Baruch 2000)

A detailed review of projections is in the "Projections of Climate, Disturbance, and Biotic Communities" section of the main text.

Other Threats and Interactions with Climate

Lizards in hot environments may be vulnerable to temperature changes associated with energetics (Sinervo and others 2010). Partly based on climate projections and temperature tolerances, Sinervo and others (2010) estimated extinction of 14% of local populations and 4% of species by 2050 for this family, Teiidae.

Although red-backed whiptail occurs in a variety of habitats, xeroriparian areas may be prone to changes associated with invasive grasses and fire occurrence. Projected increases in climate variability will also increase fire occurrence as years of high rainfall are followed by dry/hot conditions, creating conditions conducive both to fire ignition and fuel accumulation. Fire regimes in the region have also been altered by introduced plant species that provide fine fuels to carry fire. Red brome (*Bromus rubens*), Mediterranean grass (*Schismus barbatus*), and Sahara mustard (*Brassica tournefortii*) are common invasives in the region. Buffelgrass promotes a frequent high severity fire regime, which encourages further growth of these grasses while negatively impacting native desert vegetation (Williams and Baruch 2000). The vulnerability of habitats will depend on their proximity to sources of invasive grasses as well as natural fuel levels and ignition sources.

Research Needs

This species' habitat requirements are not well known. Of particular interest is its association with water sources, which, if critical, will increase vulnerability to climate change. In addition, if seasonal hibernation is triggered by photoperiod (Winne and Keck 2004), then the species may be more prone to issues related to mismatched timing between emergence and favorable temperature or resource levels.

Management Implications

Although local occurrences are not well known, activities on BMGR that impact xeroriparian areas could be detrimental to this species. Of particular management concern with climate change is the vulnerability of these habitats to severe fire, including the increased probability of invasion by exotic grass species. Shrub and tree cover may be increasingly important for thermoregulation in a warmer climate, thus activities should be managed to reduce impacts on these features.

USDA Forest Service RMRS-GTR-284. 2012.

Habitat: Red-backed whiptail (*Aspidoscelis xanthonota*)

Trait/Quality	Question	Background Info & Explanation of Score	Points
1. Area and distribution: *breeding*	Is the area or location of the associated vegetation type used for breeding activities by this species expected to change?	This species has a restricted range within Sonoran desertscrub of Arizona (Brennan and Holycross 2006). It occurs in upland Sonoran desertscrub of south central Arizona and into Mexico above 2000 ft. Associated with valley bottom floodplains, xeroriparian scrub, dunes, and various desertscrub habitats (Hall and others). Prefers rocky slopes and canyon bottoms (Brennan and Holycross 2006). No expected overall changes expected for Sonoran desertscrub and dune habitats.	0
2. Area and distribution: *non-breeding*	Is the area or location of the associated vegetation type used for non-breeding activities by this species expected to change?	Same as above.	0
3. Habitat components: *breeding*	Are specific habitat components required for breeding expected to change within associated vegetation type?	Lay eggs underground in burrows. Soils suitable for burrowing not expected to change.	0
4. Habitat components: *non-breeding*	Are other specific habitat components required for survival during non-breeding periods expected to change within associated vegetation type?	Litter and debris seems to be important for foraging and escaping predators in the canyon spotted whiptail (BISON-M), but not known if similarly important for this species.	0
5. Habitat quality	Within habitats occupied, are features of the habitat associated with better reproductive success or survival expected to change?	Presence is often associated with canyon bottoms near springs and tinajas (Brennan and Holycross 2006), which may have increased prey. Water sources expected to be reduced.	1
6. Ability to colonize new areas	What is the potential for this species to disperse?	Little information, but assumed to be highly mobile.	-1
7. Migratory or transitional habitats	Does this species require additional habitats during migration that are separated from breeding and non-breeding habitats?	No migratory habitats required.	0

Physiology: Red-backed whiptail (*Aspidoscelis xanthonota*)

Trait/Quality	Question	Background Info & Explanation of Score	Points
1. Physiological thresholds	Are limiting physiological conditions expected to change?	Heliothermic and average thermal maxima of 29 °C in this family (Sinervo and others 2010). There was no limiting factor relating to high temperature extremes for two other species of whiptails (*A. inornata* and *A. gularis*) (Winne and Keck, 2004). Assume similar tolerance for high temperatures for this species.	0
2. Sex ratio	Is sex ratio determined by temperature?	No.	0
3. Exposure to weather-related disturbance	Are disturbance events (e.g., severe storms, fires, floods) that affect survival or reproduction expected to change?	Escapes some exposure through hibernation during cold or hot months. No effects of disturbance known.	0
4. Limitations to daily activity period	Are projected temperature or precipitation regimes that influence activity period of species expected to change?	Active during spring and fall and hibernate during cold or very hot temperatures. Heliothermic and daily periods favorable for activity expected to be reduced by warmer temperatures in hot climates such as at BMGR.	1
5. Survival during resource fluctuation	Does this species have flexible strategies to cope with variation in resources across multiple years?	No strategies known.	1
6. Metabolic rates	What is this species metabolic rate?	Ectothermic.	0

Phenology: Red-backed whiptail (*Aspidoscelis xanthonota*)

Trait/Quality	Question	Background Info & Explanation of Score	Points
1. Cues	Does this species use temperature or moisture cues to initiate activities related to fecundity or survival (e.g., hibernation, migration, breeding)?	Seasonal activity patterns as related to soil temperatures were experimentally tested in whiptails. Although cessation of activities occurred during high temperatures, cessation was controlled by circadian rhythm rather than triggered by exogenous factors such as temperature or food intake (Winne and Keck 2004).	0
2. Breeding timing	Are activities related to species' fecundity or survival tied to discrete resource peaks (e.g., food, breeding sites) that are expected to change?	Lay eggs in early to mid summer (Brennan and Holycross 2006). Precipitation related to variability of food resources in *A. tigris* (Pianka 1970), and timing of precipitation is expected to change.	1

Phenology: Red-backed whiptail (*Aspidoscelis xanthonota*)

Trait/Quality	Question	Background Info & Explanation of Score	Points
3. Mismatch potential	What is the separation in time or space between cues that initiate activities related to survival or fecundity and discrete events that provide critical resources?	No direct response to resources, and initiation of breeding is not very distant from resources.	0
4. Resilience to timing mismatches during breeding	Is reproduction in this species more likely to co-occur with important events?	One reproductive event per year (Brennan and Holycross 2006).	1

Biotic Interactions: Red-backed whiptail (*Aspidoscelis xanthonota*)

Trait/Quality	Question	Background Info & Explanation of Score	Points
1. Food resources	Are important food resources for this species expected to change?	Preys on a variety of insects including ants, termites, beetles, and caterpillars, as well as spiders (Brennan and Holycross 2006). Clutch size of *A. tigris* was positively related to total precipitation of last 5 years (probably due to affect on food resources) and inversely related to variation in precipitation of last 5 years (Pianka 1970). Precipitation expected to become more variable, thereby increasing years of low food abundance.	1
2. Predators	Are important predator populations expected to change?	No information on predators, but likely various. No expected change to predation rates.	0
3. Symbionts	Are populations of symbiotic species expected to change?	No symbionts.	0
4. Disease	Is prevalence of diseases known to cause widespread mortality or reproductive failure in this species expected to change?	No known diseases.	0
5. Competitors	Are populations of important competing species expected to change?	No known competitors, although potentially other whiptails.	0

Literature Cited

Arizona Game and Fish Department. 2006. DRAFT. Arizona's comprehensive wildlife conservation strategy: 2005-2015. Arizona Game and Fish Department, Phoenix, AZ.

Asplund, K. K. 1970. Metabolic scope and body temperatures of whiptail lizards (*Cnemidophorus*). Herpetologica 26:403-411.

Bagne, K. E., M. M. Friggens, and D. M. Finch. 2011. A system for assessing vulnerability of species (SAVS) to climate change. USDA Forest Service, Rocky Mountain Research Station, Gen. Tech. Rep. RMRS-GTR-257.

Brennan, T. C. and A. T. Holycross. 2006. A Field Guide to Amphibians and Reptiles in Arizona. Arizona Game and Fish Department. Phoenix, AZ.

Esser, Gerd. 1992. Implications of climate change for production and decomposition in grasslands and coniferous forests. Ecological Applications 2:47-54.

Garfin, G. and M. Lenart. 2007. Climate change effects on Southwest water resources. Southwest Hydrology 6:16-17.

Hall, J. A., P. Comer, A. Gondor, R. Marshall, and S. Weinstein. 2001. Conservation Elements of and a Biodiversity Management Framework for the Barry M. Goldwater Range, Arizona. The Nature Conservancy of Arizona, Tucson. 199 + ix p. + 15 unpaginated figures.

Milstead, W. W. 1957. Observations on the natural history of four species of whiptail lizard, *Cnemidophorus* (Sauria, Teiidae) in Trans-Pecos Texas. Southwestern Naturalist 2:105-121.

Mitchell, D. L., D. Ivanova, R. Rabin, K. Redmond, and T.J. Brown. 2002. Gulf of California sea surface temperatures and the North American monsoon: mechanistic implications from observations. Journal of Climate 15:2261-2281.

Pianka, E. R. 1970. Comparative autecology of the lizard *Cnemidophorus tigris* in different parts of its geographic range. Ecology 51:703-720.

Rogers, G. F. and M. K. Vint. 1987. Winter precipitation and fire in the Sonoran Desert. Journal of Arid Environments 13: 47-52.

Seager, R., T. Ming, I. Held, [and others]. 2007. Model projections of an imminent transition to a more arid climate in southwestern North America. Science 316:1181-1184.

Sinervo, B., F. Méndez-de-la-Cruz, D. B. Miles, [and others]. 2010. Erosion of lizard diversity by climate change and altered thermal niches. Science 328:894-899.

Weiss, J. L. and J. T. Overpeck. 2005. Is the Sonoran Desert losing its cool? Global Change Biology 11:2065-2077.

Williams, D. G. and Z. Baruch. 2000. African grass invasion in the Americas: ecosystem consequences and the role of ecophysiology. Biological Invasions 2:213-140.

Winne, C. T. and M. B. Keck. 2004. Daily activity patterns of whiptail lizards (Squamata: Teiidae: Aspidoscelis): a proximate response to environmental conditions or an endogenous rhythm? Functional Ecology 18:314-321.

Yuman Desert Fringe-toed Lizard
(*Uma rufopunctata*)

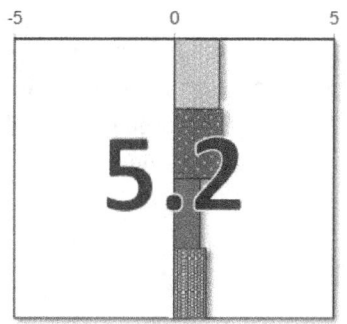

SUMMARY

Despite the fact that the Yuman desert fringe-toed lizard is adapted to a very hot and dry environment, it is vulnerable to declines associated with projected changes in climate. Vulnerability was identified for all categories, but was highest for physiological response. Management of dune habitats, including maintenance of vegetation that provides shade, will likely be important to sustaining future populations. Additionally, changes to local burrowing mammal populations may have indirect impacts and should be monitored.

VULNERABILITY	Score	Uncertainty
Habitat	1.4	29%
Physiology	1.5	17%
Phenology	0.8	0%
Interactions	1.0	60%
Overall	**5.2**	**27%**

Figure Key

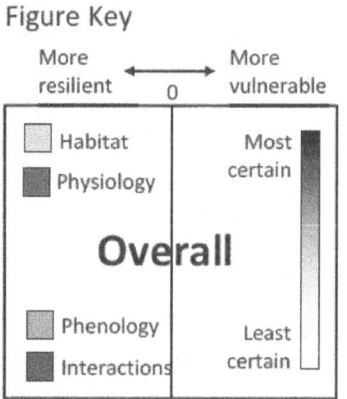

Introduction

Taxonomy has changed for this and related species leaving some confusion about designation of species. In addition, individuals from the Mohawk Dunes may be from a yet undescribed species (Trepanier and Murphy 2001). Yuman desert fringe-toed lizard was once formerly recognized as Cowles fringe-toed lizard (*Uma notata rufopunctata*) or grouped with the Sonoran fringe-toed lizard (*Uma notata*). It is listed by the Arizona Game and Fish Department as a species of greatest conservation need (AGFD 2006). Furthermore, it is identified as a species conservation element in the proposed biodiversity management framework for BMGR (Hall and others 2001).

Fringe-toed lizards are adapted to life on wind-blown sand dunes. They also occur on large sand flats and prefer habitats that are sparsely vegetated. They are found on the west section as well as the far western end of the eastern section of BMGR, particularly the Mohawk Dunes area. Regardless of the exact taxonomic relationships among species and subspecies, vulnerability scores apply to the fringe-toed lizards that occupy dune habitats at BMGR.

BMGR-East Climate and Projections

- Annual increase in temperature 2.2 °C (4 °F) by 2050 (www.climatewizard.org, A2 emissions, ensembled GCM) and greater evaporation
- No change in average rainfall by 2050 (www.climatewizard.org, A2 emissions, ensembled GCM)
- Sonoran Desert expands northward and eastward, and contracts in the southeast (Weiss and Overpeck 2005)
- More droughts and intense storms (Seager and others 2007)

- Earlier and more intense flooding (Garfin and Lenart 2007; Seager and others 2007)
- Summer monsoon changes unknown (Mitchell and others 2002)
- Grasses favored over shrubs (Esser 1992)
- Increases in invasive grasses and fires (Esser 1992; Williams and Baruch 2000)

A detailed review of projections is in the "Projections of Climate, Disturbance, and Biotic Communities" section of the main text.

Other Threats and Interactions with Climate

Dune habitats are limited and fragmented at BMGR. Invasive plants, including Saharan mustard (*Brassica tournefortii*), Arabian schismus (*Schismus arabicus*), and Mediterranean grass (*Schismus barbatas*), are encroaching on dune habitats, compromising their suitability. In addition, vehicular use of dunes, including use for military training, recreation, and law enforcement, can collapse animal burrows. Buffering of climate impacts varies with factors such as irrigation and government programs, both of which predict that drought impacts will be less severe in the United States as compared to Mexico (Vásquez-León and others 2003). In the absence of alterations to immigration policies, increased illegal traffic at the international border is expected. Barriers such as roads or fences can disrupt sand dune formation.

In an evaluation of climate change affects related to energetics, for this family, Phynosomatidae, 3% of species were identified as likely to go extinct by 2050 (Sinervo and others 2010). There may be more need for body cooling, and quality of shade may be an important factor in future suitable habitat.

Research Needs

Basic life history information is limited for this species. Research related to drought effects on lizard populations would be particularly helpful. In addition, evaluation of thermal properties of various suitable habitats would be informative for habitat management planning.

Management Implications

Management related to vehicles in fringe-toed lizard habitats will continue to be important. Planning should include the likelihood of increasing threats from vehicles and border security activities. Factors related to vegetation distribution are already known to be important for this species, but the importance of shade should further refine targeted shrub species that provide the best protection from increasing temperatures. Small burrowing mammals on dunes may be vulnerable to higher temperatures reducing availability of suitable burrows. Monitoring or management related to burrow availability may be necessary. Variability in rainfall and its association with breeding success may mean greater annual population fluctuations and, thus, greater habitat area requirements to sustain populations of this species in the future.

 USDA Forest Service RMRS-GTR-284. 2012.

Habitat: Yuman desert fringe-toed lizard (*Uma rufopunctata*)			
Trait/Quality	Question	Background Info & Explanation of Score	Points
1. Area and distribution: *breeding*	Is the area or location of the associated vegetation type used for breeding activities by this species expected to change?	Yuman fringe-toed lizards require sand habitats (either dunes or flats) that are sparsely vegetated. Occurs in dune habitats with some vegetation such as bursage and creosote (AGFD 2003). No change expected in dune area.	0
2. Area and distribution: *non-breeding*	Is the area or location of the associated vegetation type used for non-breeding activities by this species expected to change?	Same as above.	0
3. Habitat components: *breeding*	Are specific habitat components required for breeding expected to change within associated vegetation type?	Eggs are buried in moist sand (Brennan and Holycross 2006). Sand availability is not expected to change (but see Phenology, Question 2)	0
4. Habitat components: *non-breeding*	Are other specific habitat components required for survival during non-breeding periods expected to change within associated vegetation type?	Burrows in sand to escape predators and is more likely to occur in areas with more sand and less vegetation, but require some vegetation for predator escape and thermoregulation (Pough 1970). Vegetation that provides suitable shade is expected to be reduced with increasing droughts. Burrows also required for hibernation (see Interactions, Question 3)	1
5. Habitat quality	Within habitats occupied, are features of the habitat associated with better reproductive success or survival expected to change?	Species presence is associated with greater quantities of sand, but unknown connection to survival though potentially allows for better escape from predators.	0
6. Ability to colonize new areas	What is the potential for this species to disperse?	Little information. Probably have fairly limited movements and may be restricted by patchiness of dune habitats.	1
7. Migratory or transitional habitats	Does this species require additional habitats during migration that are separated from breeding and non-breeding habitats?	Not migratory.	0

Physiology: Yuman desert fringe-toed lizard (*Uma rufopunctata*)

Trait/Quality	Question	Background Info & Explanation of Score	Points
1. Physiological thresholds	Are limiting physiological conditions expected to change?	This species already experiences very high temperatures. Species in this family may be prone to extinction based on body temperatures and activity restrictions imposed by hot temperatures (Sinervo and others 2010).	1
2. Sex ratio	Is sex ratio determined by temperature?	No.	0
3. Exposure to weather-related disturbance	Are disturbance events (e.g., severe storms, fires, floods) that affect survival or reproduction expected to change?	Hibernates underground in existing burrows during the cold months of winter and late fall (AGFD 2003), thus may escape many storms. No known mortality factors with disturbance.	0
4. Limitations to daily activity period	Are projected temperature or precipitation regimes that influence activity period of species expected to change?	Requires vegetation for shade, so prone to increasing need to use shade on hot days, thus reducing active periods.	1
5. Survival during resource fluctuation	Does this species have flexible strategies to cope with variation in resources across multiple years?	None known.	1
6. Metabolic rates	What is this species metabolic rate?	Ectothermic.	-1

Phenology: Yuman desert fringe-toed lizard (*Uma rufopunctata*)

Trait/Quality	Question	Background Info & Explanation of Score	Points
1. Cues	Does this species use temperature or moisture cues to initiate activities related to fecundity or survival (e.g., hibernation, migration, breeding)?	Temperature affects emergence from hibernation, egg development, and surface activity (AZGFD 2003). Photoperiod was more important than temperature in determining egg laying in *Uma notata* (Mayhew 1961). Hibernation timing is vulnerable to changes in temperature.	1
2. Breeding timing	Are activities related to species' fecundity or survival tied to discrete resource peaks (e.g., food, breeding sites) that are expected to change?	Lay eggs from May through August (AGFD 2003). Eggs are buried in moist sand (Brennan and Holycross 2006). Moist periods will likely change as seasonal rainfall shifts.	1
3. Mismatch potential	What is the separation in time or space between cues that initiate activities related to survival or fecundity and discrete events that provide critical resources?	No large distance between breeding and resources.	0

Phenology: Yuman desert fringe-toed lizard (*Uma rufopunctata*)

Trait/Quality	Question	Background Info & Explanation of Score	Points
4. Resilience to timing mismatches during breeding	Is reproduction in this species more likely to co-occur with important events?	Females may lay more than one clutch per year, but forego reproduction when food is scarce (Mayhew 1966).	-1

Biotic Interactions: Yuman desert fringe-toed lizard (*Uma rufopunctata*)

Trait/Quality	Question	Background Info & Explanation of Score	Points
1. Food resources	Are important food resources for this species expected to change?	Omnivorous and eat a wide variety of insects and vegetation (Turner and Schwalbe 1998). No reproduction occurs in years with low invertebrate abundance, thus these types of foods are limiting to populations. All invertebrate prey are not likely to decline or increase simultaneously.	0
2. Predators	Are important predator populations expected to change?	Likely various birds and mammals. No overall changes expected.	0
3. Symbionts	Are populations of symbiotic species expected to change?	Requires other animals to create burrows for hibernation. Uses animal burrows for hibernation (AGFD 2003). Fewer burrowing mammals may occupy these habitats as they get hotter.	1
4. Disease	Is prevalence of diseases known to cause widespread mortality or reproductive failure in this species expected to change?	None known.	0
5. Competitors	Are populations of important competing species expected to change?	None known.	0

Literature Cited

Arizona Game and Fish Department. 2003. *Uma rufopunctata*. Unpublished abstract compiled and edited by the Heritage Data Management System, Arizona Game and Fish Department, Phoenix, AZ.

Arizona Game and Fish Department. 2006. DRAFT. Arizona's comprehensive wildlife conservation strategy: 2005-2015. Arizona Game and Fish Department, Phoenix, AZ.

Bagne, K. E., M. M. Friggens, and D. M. Finch. 2011. A system for assessing vulnerability of species (SAVS) to climate change. USDA Forest Service, Rocky Mountain Research Station, Gen. Tech. Rep. RMRS-GTR-257.

Brennan, T. C., and A. T. Holycross. 2006. A field guide to amphibians and reptiles in Arizona. Arizona Game and Fish Department. Phoenix, AZ.

Esser, Gerd. 1992. Implications of climate change for production and decomposition in grasslands and coniferous forests. Ecological Applications 2:47-54.

Garfin, G. and M. Lenart. 2007. Climate change effects on Southwest water resources. Southwest Hydrology 6:16-17.

Hall, J. A., P. Comer, A. Gondor, R. Marshall, and S. Weinstein. 2001. Conservation Elements of and a Biodiversity Management Framework for the Barry M. Goldwater Range, Arizona. The Nature Conservancy of Arizona, Tucson.

Mayhew, W. 1961. Photoperiodic response in female fringe-toed lizards. Science 134:2104-2105.

Mayhew, W. W. 1966. Reproduction in the psammophilous lizard *Uma scoparia*. Copeia 1:114-122.

Mitchell, D. L., D. Ivanova, R. Rabin, K. Redmond, and T. J. Brown. 2002. Gulf of California sea surface temperatures and the North American monsoon: mechanistic implications from observations. Journal of Climate 15:2261-2281.

Pough, F. H. 1970. The burrowing ecology of the sand lizard, *Uma notata*. Copeia: 1970:145-157.

Seager, R., T. Ming, and I. Held, [and others]. 2007. Model projections of an imminent transition to a more arid climate in southwestern North America. Science 316:1181-1184.

Trepanier, T. L. and R. W. Murphy. 2001. The Coachella Valley fringe-toed lizard (*Uma inornata*): genetic diversity and phylogenetic relationships of an endangered species. Molecular Phylogenetics and Evolution 18:327-334.

Turner, D. S. and C. R. Schwalbe. 1998. Ecology of Cowles fringe-toed lizard. Arizona Game and Fish Department Heritage Fund IIPAM Project No. I95042. Final Report to Arizona Game and Fish Department. 78 p.

Vásquez-León, Marcela, C. T. West, and T. J. Finan. 2003. A comparative assessment of climate vulnerability: agriculture and ranching on both sides of the US-Mexico border. Global Environmental Change 13:159-173.

Weiss, J. L. and J. T. Overpeck. 2005. Is the Sonoran Desert losing its cool? Global Change Biology 11:2065-2077.

Williams, D. G. and Z. Baruch. 2000. African grass invasion in the Americas: ecosystem consequences and the role of ecophysiology. Biological Invasions 2:213-140.

American Peregrine Falcon
(*Falco peregrinus anatum*)

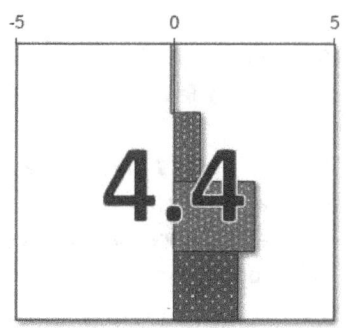

SUMMARY

Peregrine falcons are flexible in their habitat use, which will help them cope with climate change effects to some extent. Phenology, as related to prey levels, is an area of potential vulnerability depending on whether different aspects shift in concert. Although Arizona habitats are expected to remain suitable in the near future, the falcons will be exposed to other climate change effects at wintering and stopover sites. If falcons are found breeding, any restriction of military activities near nesting sites needs to consider future breeding timing changes.

VULNERABILITY	Score	Uncertainty
Habitat	**-0.1**	0%
Physiology	**0.8**	33%
Phenology	**2.5**	25%
Interactions	**2.0**	20%
Overall	**4.4**	**18%**

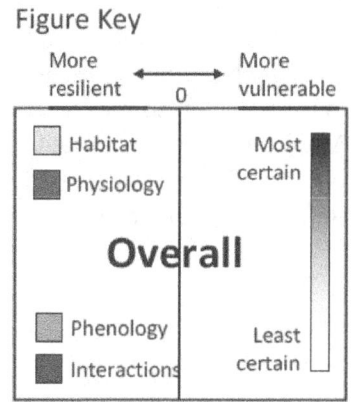

Introduction
Peregrine falcons are not known to nest on BMGR and may only be transients. The species was Federally listed in 1970 and delisted in 1999. However, the Arizona Game and Fish Department designated the American peregrine falcon as a species of greatest conservation need, Tier 1B, in the Arizona State Wildlife Action Plan (AGFD 2006).

BMGR-East Climate and Projections
- Annual increase in temperature 2.2 °C (4 °F) by 2050 (www.climatewizard.org, A2 emissions, ensembled GCM) and greater evaporation
- No change in average rainfall by 2050 (www.climatewizard.org, A2 emissions, ensembled GCM)
- Sonoran Desert expands northward and eastward, and contracts in the southeast (Weiss and Overpeck 2005)
- More droughts and intense storms (Seager and others 2007)
- Earlier and more intense flooding (Garfin and Lenart 2007; Seager and others 2007)
- Summer monsoon changes unknown (Mitchell and others 2002)
- Grasses favored over shrubs (Esser 1992)
- Increases in invasive grasses and fires (Esser 1992; Williams and Baruch 2000)
- Warmer temperatures and decreased soil moisture in Mexico (Liverman and O'Brien 1991)
- Decreased annual rainfall in Central America (Magrin and others 2007)

A detailed review of projections is in the "Projections of Climate, Disturbance, and Biotic Communities" section of the main text.

Other Threats and Interactions with Climate

Population declines in the past are thought to have been primarily due to DDT use, and populations are recovering. Because this species is migratory, climate or land-use changes in Mexico and Central America will affect populations in Arizona.

Research Needs

Wintering habitat requirements for this species are not well known. Migration routes and destinations are also not well known for populations in the southwest United States. In addition, physiological thresholds as they relate to increasing temperatures in hotter portions of the falcon's range are needed to predict climate change response.

Management Implications

Territory size and spacing is related to nest site and prey availability (White and others 2002). Both are probably relatively low in this region, thus it is unlikely that management actions will affect more than a few individuals. Peregrine falcons drink frequently (White and others 2002), and water needs will likely increase in the future, thus management related to water sources, including artificial waters, will be important. Monitoring and identification of suitable nesting habitats will indicate if further measures need to be taken. If nesting is confirmed, restriction of activities at suitable nesting sites is important and managers should plan for shifts in breeding timing.

Habitat: American peregrine falcon (*Falco peregrinus anatum*)			
Trait/Quality	**Question**	**Background Info & Explanation of Score**	**Points**
1. Area and distribution: *breeding*	Is the area or location of the associated vegetation type used for breeding activities by this species expected to change?	Occupies a wide variety of habitats, including forests, grasslands, and scrublands (White and others 2002). Most of BMGR has suitable vegetation and should continue to remain suitable despite changes in dominance of specific vegetation types.	**0**
2. Area and distribution: *non-breeding*	Is the area or location of the associated vegetation type used for non-breeding activities by this species expected to change?	Occupies even wider range of habitats in winter. No expected changes.	**0**
3. Habitat components: *breeding*	Are specific habitat components required for breeding expected to change within associated vegetation type?	Vertical substrate with ledges for nesting. Mostly cliffs, but will also use buildings in urban areas. No projected changes to cliffs.	**0**
4. Habitat components: *non-breeding*	Are other specific habitat components required for survival during non-breeding periods expected to change within associated vegetation type?	Uses perches to scan for prey. Wide variety of perch locations with no expected change in availability.	**0**
5. Habitat quality	Within habitats occupied, are features of the habitat associated with better reproductive success or survival expected to change?	Reproductive success has been related to female age, but not habitat variables (White and others 2002).	**0**
6. Ability to colonize new areas	What is the potential for this species to disperse?	Highly mobile.	**-1**
7. Migratory or transitional habitats	Does this species require additional habitats during migration that are separated from breeding and non-breeding habitats?	Migratory. Birds that breed in more southerly locations may actually travel less south into Mexico than those that breed in the far north, which may travel to Central America to winter (White and others 2002).	**1**

Physiology: American peregrine falcon (*Falco peregrinus anatum*)

Trait/Quality	Question	Background Info & Explanation of Score	Points
1. Physiological thresholds	Are limiting physiological conditions expected to change?	One of the most widely distributed vertebrate species, peregrine falcons are tolerant of a wide range of conditions (White and others 2002). Convective cooling through the bare tarsus is considered important, and this surface area varies with region (White and others 2002). Not expected to be limited, although no specific information.	0
2. Sex ratio	Is sex ratio determined by temperature?	No.	0
3. Exposure to weather-related disturbance	Are disturbance events (e.g., severe storms, fires, floods) that affect survival or reproduction expected to change?	Thought to be less prone to mortality from adverse weather during migration than many other bird species (White and others 2002). Nestlings vulnerable to late, wet springs (White and others 2002). Spring expected to occur earlier rather than later, although this may not be a major factor in warmer climates.	0
4. Limitations to daily activity period	Are projected temperature or precipitation regimes that influence activity period of species expected to change?	Most cooling is through behaviors such as orientation, erection of feathers, or panting. No known limitations to daily active period.	0
5. Survival during resource fluctuation	Does this species have flexible strategies to cope with variation in resources across multiple years?	None known. Only rare records of cooperative breeding (White and others 2002).	1
6. Metabolic rates	What is this species metabolic rate?	Moderate endothermic, although higher than congeneric species (White and others 2002).	0

Phenology: American peregrine falcon (*Falco peregrinus anatum*)

Trait/Quality	Question	Background Info & Explanation of Score	Points
1. Cues	Does this species use temperature or moisture cues to initiate activities related to fecundity or survival (e.g., hibernation, migration, breeding)?	Timing of migration and breeding seems to be in response to a wide variety of signals, including climate, photoperiod, and prey levels (White and others 2002). Not a direct response to temperature alone.	0
2. Breeding timing	Are activities related to species' fecundity or survival tied to discrete resource peaks (e.g., food, breeding sites) that are expected to change?	Based on areas with similar climates, egg laying occurs from March to April (White and others 2002). Likely that breeding is timed to prey levels that fluctuate with breeding of other species, which, in turn, is subject to climate-related changes.	1

Phenology: American peregrine falcon (*Falco peregrinus anatum*)			
Trait/Quality	Question	Background Info & Explanation of Score	Points
3. Mismatch potential	What is the separation in time or space between cues that initiate activities related to survival or fecundity and discrete events that provide critical resources?	In some areas, migratory behaviors seem to be in direct response to prey levels (White and others 2002). This seems to be limited to leaving breeding grounds, and breeding timing is not likely to be very flexible to resource timing.	0
4. Resilience to timing mismatches during breeding	Is reproduction in this species more likely to co-occur with important events?	One brood per year.	1

Biotic Interactions: American peregrine falcon (*Falco peregrinus anatum*)			
Trait/Quality	Question	Background Info & Explanation of Score	Points
1. Food resources	Are important food resources for this species expected to change?	Most important prey are birds although a wide variety of species from various taxonomic groups are also eaten (White and others 2002). Doves are likely important prey in this region and may decline with shrinking water sources.	1
2. Predators	Are important predator populations expected to change?	Great horned owls are an important predator on young, but predation for adults is probably not frequent. No expected changes in predation levels.	0
3. Symbionts	Are populations of symbiotic species expected to change?	No symbionts.	0
4. Disease	Is prevalence of diseases known to cause widespread mortality or reproductive failure in this species expected to change?	Some secondary infection through prey of *Trichomonas* (White and others 2002). Infections may increase with increased transmission in doves from crowding at shrinking water sources.	1
5. Competitors	Are populations of important competing species expected to change?	No major competitors known.	0

Literature Cited

Arizona Game and Fish Department. 2006. DRAFT. Arizona's comprehensive wildlife conservation strategy: 2005-2015. Arizona Game and Fish Department, Phoenix, AZ.

Bagne, K. E., M. M. Friggens, and D. M. Finch. 2011. A system for assessing vulnerability of species (SAVS) to climate change. USDA Forest Service, Rocky Mountain Research Station, Gen. Tech. Rep. RMRS-GTR-257.

Esser, G. 1992. Implications of climate change for production and decomposition in grasslands and coniferous forests. Ecological Applications 2:47-54.

Garfin, G. and M. Lenart. 2007. Climate change effects on Southwest water resources. Southwest Hydrology 6:16-17.

Liverman, D. M. and K. L. O'Brien. 1991. Global Warming and Climate Change in Mexico. Pages 351-364 In Global Environmental Change. Butterworth-Heinemann Ltd.

Magrin, G., C. G. García, D. Cruz Choque, J. C. Giménez, A. R. Moreno, G. J. Nagy, C. Nobre, and A. Villamizar. 2007. Latin America. Pages 581-615 In M. L. Parry, O. F. Canziani, J. P. Palutikof, P. J. van der Linden, and C. E. Hanson, eds., Climate Change 2007: Impacts, Adaptation and Vulnerability. Contribution of Working Group II to the Fourth Assessment Report of the Intergovernmental Panel on Climate Change. Cambridge University Press, Cambridge, UK.

Mitchell, D. L., D. Ivanova, R. Rabin, K. Redmond, and T. J. Brown. 2002. Gulf of California sea surface temperatures and the North American monsoon: Mechanistic implications from observations. Journal of Climate 15:2261-2281.

Scholze, M., W. Knorr, N. W. Arnell, and I. C. Prentice. 2005. A climate change risk analysis for world ecosystems. Proceedings of the National Academy of Sciences 103:13116-13120.

Seager, R., T. Ming, I. Held, [and others]. 2007. Model projections of an imminent transition to a more arid climate in southwestern North America. Science 316:1181-1184.

Weiss, J. L. and J. T. Overpeck. 2005. Is the Sonoran Desert losing its cool? Global Change Biology 11:2065-2077.

White, C. M., N. J. Clum, T. J. Cade, and W. G. Hunt. 2002. Peregrine Falcon (*Falco peregrinus*). In A. Poole, ed., The Birds of North America Online. Ithaca: Cornell Lab of Ornithology.

Williams, D. G. and Z. Baruch. 2000. African grass invasion in the Americas: ecosystem consequences and the role of ecophysiology. Biological Invasions 2:213-140.

Cactus Ferruginous Pygmy-Owl
(*Glaucidium brasilianum cactorum*)

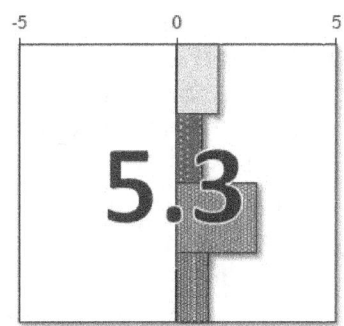

SUMMARY

The cactus ferruginous pygmy-owl is vulnerable to declines associated with a warming climate. Vulnerabilities are associated with changes expected for xeroriparian habitats and interactions with other cavity nesting species. In addition, this species possesses few resilient traits that could help it cope with changing conditions. Management related to fire and to both plant and animal invasive species will be important.

VULNERABILITY	Score	Uncertainty
Habitat	**1.3**	100%
Physiology	**0.8**	33%
Phenology	**2.5**	50%
Interactions	**1.0**	60%
Overall	**5.3**	64%

Figure Key

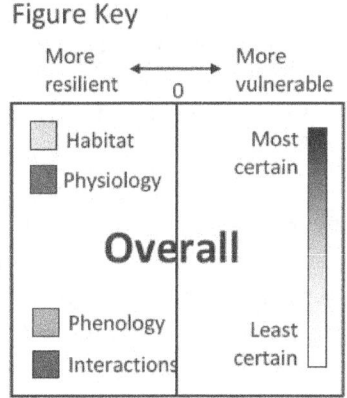

Introduction

The cactus ferruginous pygmy-owl is a subspecies of the ferruginous pygmy-owl. This subspecies occurs at the northern end of the species' distribution, which reaches all the way to Tierra del Fuego (Cartron and others 2000). The Arizona population was listed as a distinct population segment until 2006, when it was determined that this designation was unsupported (Federal Register/Vol. 71/April 14, 2006). It was listed in Arizona as Federally endangered in 1997 after apparent population declines. As of June 2008, the USFWS determined a review of the status of this subspecies was warranted and initiated a status review (Federal Register/Vol. 73/June 2, 2008). The petition for this status review identified populations in the western United States as distinct and as *Glaucidium ridgwayi cactorum* (*G. brasilianum* being restricted to South America) (Proudfoot and others 2006). The findings of this review were not available at the time of this report. The USFWS found that listing was not warranted for the entire species range or as distinct population segments (Federal Register/Vol. 76/Oct. 5, 2011). The State of Arizona identifies this as a species of greatest conservation need, Tier 1A (AGFD 2006). Population declines may have begun as early as the 1920s and are likely related to loss and degradation of riparian habitats (Johnson and others 2003). Populations remain low and fragmented in Arizona. The only other U.S. occurrences are in Texas where populations are not proposed for Federal listing and may be from a different subspecies.

Cactus ferruginous pygmy-owls occur in Organ Pipe Cactus National Monument, Cabeza Prieta National Wildlife Refuge, and on Tohono O'odham Nation lands (USFWS 2003). They are not recorded on BMGR as of the time of this report but have the potential to occur, particularly in the Sauceda and Sand Tanks Mountains (Hall and others 2001), and there have been several unconfirmed sightings on BMGR (USFWS 2003).

BMGR-East Climate and Projections

- Annual increase in temperature 2.2 °C (4 °F) by 2050 (www.climatewizard.org, A2 emissions, ensembled GCM) and greater evaporation
- No change in average rainfall by 2050 (www.climatewizard.org, A2 emissions, ensembled GCM)
- Sonoran Desert expands northward and eastward, and contracts in the southeast (Weiss and Overpeck 2005)
- More droughts and intense storms (Seager and others 2007)
- Earlier and more intense flooding (Garfin and Lenart 2007; Seager and others 2007)
- Summer monsoon changes unknown (Mitchell and others 2002)
- Grasses favored over shrubs (Esser 1992)
- Increases in invasive grasses and fires (Esser 1992; Williams and Baruch 2000)
- CAM plants (succulents and cacti) will be resilient to increasing temperatures (Smith and others 1984)

A detailed review of projections is in the "Projections of Climate, Disturbance, and Biotic Communities" section of the main text.

Other Threats and Interactions with Climate

Destruction of riparian woodlands in Arizona is likely to have played a significant role in the decline of this species (Johnson and others 1979), and continued degradation of these habitats is of concern. Changes in hydrologic regimes and warmer temperatures along with increased wildfires and human demands for water with climate change will only increase the threat to the species' habitat. Individuals are also susceptible to injury or death from collisions with traffic (USFWS 2003). In addition, they may abandon nests or alter movements in response to disturbance (USFWS 2003), including disturbance associated with military activities.

Projected increases in climate variability will increase fire occurrence as years of high rainfall are followed by dry/hot conditions, creating conditions conducive both to fire ignition and fuel accumulation. Although some level of fire occurrence may be beneficial to ferruginous pygmy-owl habitats, fires that are intense enough to kill plants used for nesting or encourage conversion to other habitat types will be detrimental. Fire regimes in the region have also been altered by introduced plant species that provide fine fuels to carry fire. Red brome (*Bromus rubens*), Mediterranean grass (*Schismus barbatus*), and Sahara mustard (*Brassica tournefortii*) are common invasives in the region. Buffelgrass (*Pennisetum ciliare*) promotes a frequent high severity fire regime, which encourages further growth of grasses while negatively impacting native desert vegetation (Williams and Baruch 2000).

Research Needs

In general, there is only limited information about the life history and population demographics of the species, particularly from outside the United States. Little is known about the habitat quality of locations where pygmy-owls are found (Cartron and others 2000c), but this would provide valuable information for conservation. Also, information is needed on responses to land management practices such as grazing and recreation. For example, is installation of nest boxes a viable option for sustaining populations (Cartron and others 2000c)? Information is needed on limiting factors at the northern range boundary and dispersal behaviors, which is important for determining the potential for population increase or range expansion in the United States (Proudfoot and others 2000). Investigation into the factors involved in the apparent shift in habitat use from riparian woodlands to desert scrub may also shed light on the species' potential response to changing climatic conditions. Studies of basic ecological and physiological information could be more successful in locations where populations are larger. The USFWS (2003) noted that information about populations in Mexico and their interaction with populations in Arizona is critical to understanding the degree of isolation of the U.S. population and management needs. The owl's interactions with other species are also poorly understood.

Management Implications

Management actions that protect large trees and saguaros while promoting understory growth should favor the ferruginous pygmy-owl. Management of introduction and spread of invasive grasses will also be important. Invasive grasses can degrade xeroriparian habitats as well as encourage fires, which will remove important shrubs and trees for this species. Management related to control of invasive grasses will be especially important as desert washes will be prone to invasion. Careful use of prescribed fire may enhance habitat suitability (USFWS 2003) and may protect habitats from more severe fires.

Post-fire rehabilitation of habitats is also an important management planning consideration as high severity fires will be inevitable. Nest boxes could mitigate some loss of trees or cactus, but attention should be given to box microclimate during construction and placement. Although active management of competing non-native cavity nesters may not be necessary, care should be taken to not enhance habitats for these species.

Habitat: Cactus ferruginous pygmy-owl (*Glaucidium brasilianum cactorum*)

Trait/Quality	Question	Background Info & Explanation of Score	Points
1. Area and distribution: *breeding*	Is the area or location of the associated vegetation type used for breeding activities by this species expected to change?	In Arizona, the cactus ferruginous pygmy owl occurs in Sonoran desert scrub and xeroriparian vegetation, but historically was also associated with cottonwood and mesquite riparian woodlands (Cartron and others 2000b). Desert scrub habitats may be of marginal quality, but may play an important role in habitat connectivity. A complex landscape of edges, dense shrubs, and open overstory seems to be important. Habitat requirements are not well known. Although desert scrub will likely remain, xeroriparian habitats with trees and shrubs will be more vulnerable to declines associated with water table declines as well as increasing fires.	1
2. Area and distribution: *non-breeding*	Is the area or location of the associated vegetation type used for non-breeding activities by this species expected to change?	Same as above.	1
3. Habitat components: *breeding*	Are specific habitat components required for breeding expected to change within associated vegetation type?	Trees or cactus large enough to support cavities are required for breeding. Saguaro cactus are commonly used nesting substrates in Arizona (Cartron and others 2000b). Require suitable substrate for nesting cavities. Dependent on excavating species (see Interactions). Large trees are prone to fire and drought. Cactus are likely more resilient and often occupy habitats less prone to fire (but see other threats). Nests located 1996-2002 in Arizona were primarily in saguaro cactus.	0
4. Habitat components: *non-breeding*	Are other specific habitat components required for survival during non-breeding periods expected to change within associated vegetation type?	Cavities are also used for caching prey, so number of cavities may be associated with habitat selection (Proudfoot and others 2000). Same as above.	0
5. Habitat quality	Within habitats occupied, are features of the habitat associated with better reproductive success or survival expected to change?	Seem to be associated with proximity to forest patches and edges of open woodlands (USFWS 2003). Understory cover may be important for survival, particularly of fledglings (USFWS 2003). It is not known if fires have a positive or negative effect on habitat for this species (USFWS 2003), although throughout its range, it occurs in second growth shrublands, forest edge habitats, and xeroriparian habitats (Cartron and others 2000b). Drier conditions will likely reduce foliar cover and increase shrub mortality.	1
6. Ability to colonize new areas	What is the potential for this species to disperse?	Generally considered to be permanent resident with dispersal of juveniles, but there has been some suggestion of possible migratory behaviors from Sonora, Mexico (Proudfoot and others 2000; USFWS 2003). Juveniles may disperse more than 20 km (USFWS 2003). Little information is available on site fidelity (Proudfoot and others 2000). Highly mobile species with most dispersal by juveniles of both sexes.	-1

Habitat: Cactus ferruginous pygmy-owl (*Glaucidium brasilianum cactorum*)

Trait/Quality	Question	Background Info & Explanation of Score	Points
7. Migratory or transitional habitats	Does this species require additional habitats during migration that are separated from breeding and non-breeding habitats?	Does not require transitional habitats, although movements are not well studied (see above).	0

Physiology: Cactus ferruginous pygmy-owl (*Glaucidium brasilianum cactorum*)

Trait/Quality	Question	Background Info & Explanation of Score	Points
1. Physiological thresholds	Are limiting physiological conditions expected to change?	Arizona is the northern edge of the range for this species (USFWS 2003) and may be less suitable than more southerly and tropical parts of the range (Johnson and others 2003). Although this species lives in a broad spectrum of physical conditions, does not possess specialized adaptations for desert conditions. Very hot environments, such as BMGR, may exceed tolerances in the future.	1
2. Sex ratio	Is sex ratio determined by temperature?	No.	0
3. Exposure to weather-related disturbance	Are disturbance events (e.g., severe storms, fires, floods) that affect survival or reproduction expected to change?	No information.	0
4. Limitations to daily activity period	Are projected temperature or precipitation regimes that influence activity period of species expected to change?	These owls are active primarily during the day, particularly at dawn and dusk, but also can be active at night (Proudfoot and Johnson 2000). Night activity was drastically reduced 4-7 days before initiation of fledging (Proudfoot and Johnson 2000). No known correspondence of activity with climate.	0
5. Survival during resource fluctuation	Does this species have flexible strategies to cope with variation in resources across multiple years?	None known, although flexible migratory behaviors are potentially helpful if present.	0
6. Metabolic rates	What is this species metabolic rate?	Moderate endothermic.	0

Phenology: Cactus ferruginous pygmy-owl (*Glaucidium brasilianum cactorum*)

Trait/Quality	Question	Background Info & Explanation of Score	Points
1. Cues	Does this species use temperature or moisture cues to initiate activities related to fecundity or survival (e.g., hibernation, migration, breeding)?	Probably use combination of internal and external signals to initiate breeding.	0
2. Breeding timing	Are activities related to species' fecundity or survival tied to discrete resource peaks (e.g., food, breeding sites) that are expected to change?	Mating begins in February with egg laying in late April to May. Young fledge from the end of May through June and disperse from natal sites end of July through August (Proudfoot and others 2000). Breeding likely timed to coincide with peak food availability or favorable climate. Discrete events not specifically known, but prey species often subject to temperature-related fluctuations.	1
3. Mismatch potential	What is the separation in time or space between cues that initiate activities related to survival or fecundity and discrete events that provide critical resources?	Discrete events not known, but not likely to respond directly to resource levels.	0
4. Resilience to timing mismatches during breeding	Is reproduction in this species more likely to co-occur with important events?	One breeding event, and re-nesting only occurs if failure occurs very early in the nesting cycle.	1

Biotic Interactions: Cactus ferruginous pygmy-owl (*Glaucidium brasilianum cactorum*)

Trait/Quality	Question	Background Info & Explanation of Score	Points
1. Food resources	Are important food resources for this species expected to change?	Prey items include birds, lizards, insects, and small mammals, which can be larger than the pygmy-owl. Reptiles are the primary prey in Arizona (Cartron and others 2000). May be preyed upon by larger raptors, but there are few documented cases of predation (USFWS 2003). Reptiles are an important component of the diet, but various species are taken along with alternative prey such as insects and small mammals. No overall changes expected in prey.	0
2. Predators	Are important predator populations expected to change?	Important predators include other larger raptors. Predation is not likely a major source of mortality.	0
3. Symbionts	Are populations of symbiotic species expected to change?	Needs other species to excavate cavities. Gila woodpeckers and northern flicker are common excavators of the cavities used by the pygmy-owl (Cartron and others 2000). A wide variety of other secondary cavity nesters compete for cavities, including non-native species such as European starlings and house sparrows,	0

Biotic Interactions: Cactus ferruginous pygmy-owl (*Glaucidium brasilianum cactorum*)

Trait/Quality	Question	Background Info & Explanation of Score	Points
		but these interactions are not well studied (USFWS 2003). Generally uses cavities created by Gila woodpeckers and northern flickers, but not limited to these species. Gila woodpeckers were assessed as relatively neutral to climate change at BMGR.	
4. Disease	Is prevalence of diseases known to cause widespread mortality or reproductive failure in this species expected to change?	May be susceptible to trichomoniasis, which is transmitted from infected prey (Cartron and others 2000). West Nile virus may also affect this species (USFWS 2003), but no records. Trichomoniasis is present in Arizona and could be passed through infected mourning doves or pigeons. Not expected to be a significant source of mortality as these are not common prey items. Transmission of West Nile virus from mosquitoes may be reduced during drier conditions, but not a known mortality factor in this species.	0
5. Competitors	Are populations of important competing species expected to change?	Competes for cavities with other species. General outcome of these encounters is unknown. Non-natives such as starlings and house finches likely compete for cavities and are likely resilient to climate change.	1

Literature Cited

Arizona Game and Fish Department. 2006. DRAFT. Arizona's comprehensive wildlife conservation strategy: 2005-2015. Arizona Game and Fish Department, Phoenix, AZ.

Bagne, K. E., M. M. Friggens, and D. M. Finch. 2011. A system for assessing vulnerability of species (SAVS) to climate change. USDA Forest Service, Rocky Mountain Research Station, Gen. Tech. Rep. RMRS-GTR-257.

Cartron, J. E., W. S. Richardson, and G. A. Proudfoot. 2000. The cactus ferruginous pygmy-owl: taxonomy, distribution, and natural history. Pages 5-16 In J.E. Cartron, D. Finch, tech. eds., Ecology and conservation of the cactus ferruginous pygmy-owl in Arizona. USDA Forest Service, Rocky Mountain Research Station, Gen. Tech. Rep. RMRS-GTR-43.

Cartron, J. E., S. H. Stoleson, S. M. Russell, G. A. Proudfoot, and W. S. Richardson. 2000b. The ferruginous pygmy-owl in the tropics and at the northern end of its range: habitat relations and requirements. Pages 47-55 In J. E. Cartron, D. M. Finch, tech. eds., Ecology and conservation of the cactus ferruginous pygmy-owl in Arizona. USDA Forest Service, Rocky Mountain Research Station, Gen. Tech. Rep. RMRS-GTR-43.

Cartron, J. E., W. S. Richardson, D. M. Finch, and D. J. Krueper. 2000c. Research needs for the conservation of the cactus ferruginous pygmy-owl in Arizona. Pages 65-68 In J. E. Cartron, D. M. Finch, tech. eds., Ecology and conservation of the cactus ferruginous pygmy-owl in Arizona. USDA Forest Service, Rocky Mountain Research Station, Gen. Tech. Rep. RMRS-GTR-43.

Hall, J. A., P. Comer, A. Gondor, R. Marshall, and S. Weinstein. 2001. Conservation Elements of and a Biodiversity Management Framework for the Barry M. Goldwater Range, Arizona. The Nature Conservancy of Arizona, Tucson.

Johnson, R. R., J. E. Cartron, L. T. Haight, R. B. Duncan, and K. J. Kingsley. 2003. Cactus ferruginous pygmy-owl in Arizona, 1872-1971. The Southwestern Naturalist 48:389-401.

Monson, G. 1998. Ferruginous Pygmy-Owl (*Glaucidium brasilianum*). Pages 159-161 In R. L. Glinski, ed., The Raptors of Arizona. University of Arizona Press, Tucson.

Mitchell, D. L., D. Ivanova, R. Rabin, K. Redmond, and T. J. Brown. 2002. Gulf of California sea surface temperatures and the North American monsoon: mechanistic implications from observations. Journal of Climate 15:2261-2281.

Proudfoot, G. A. and R. R. Johnson. 2000. Ferruginous Pygmy-Owl (*Glaucidium brasilianum*). In A. Poole, ed., The Birds of North America Online. Ithaca: Cornell Lab of Ornithology.

Proudfoot, G. A., R. L. Honeycutt, and R. D. Slack. 2006. Mitochondrial DNA variation and phylogeography of the ferruginous pygmy-owl (*Glaucidium brasilianum*). Conservation Genetics 7:1-12.

Seager, R., T. Ming, I. Held, [and others]. 2007. Model projections of an imminent transition to a more arid climate in southwestern North America. Science 316:1181-1184.

U.S. Fish and Wildlife Service (USFWS). 2003. Cactus ferruginous pygmy-owl (*Glaucidium brasilianum cactorum*) draft recovery plan. Albuquerque, NM. 164 p. + appendices.

Weiss, J. L. and J. T. Overpeck. 2005. Is the Sonoran Desert losing its cool? Global Change Biology 11:2065-2077.

Williams, D. G., and Z. Baruch. 2000. African grass invasion in the Americas: ecosystem consequences and the role of ecophysiology. Biological Invasions 2:213-140.

Gilded Flicker
(*Colaptes chrysoides*)

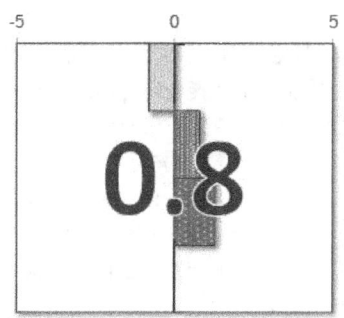

SUMMARY

Gilded flicker was not found to be particularly vulnerable to declines associated with projected climate change. Although not widespread at BMGR, expansion of buffelgrass threatens to convert saguaro-dominated habitats to grasslands and greatly reduce habitat available for the gilded flicker. Management related to sustaining populations of saguaro will be important to the future of this species. Control of invasive grasses will also be important for reducing high intensity fires, preventing conversion to grasslands, and, possibly, sustaining ant populations.

VULNERABILITY	Score	Uncertainty
Habitat	**-0.8**	43%
Physiology	**0.8**	50%
Phenology	**1.3**	50%
Interactions	**0.0**	40%
Overall	**0.8**	45%

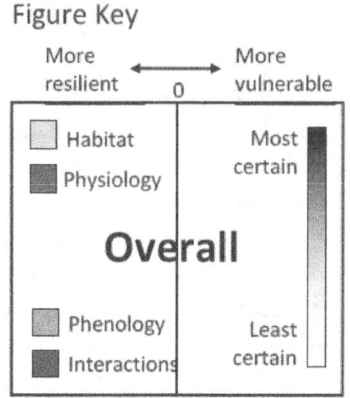

Introduction
Gilded flickers are endemic to the Sonoran desert. It is one of several species that make up the primary excavator guild identified as a conservation element for the biodiversity management framework (Hall and others 2001). A wide range of other species use cavities excavated by the gilded flicker. In addition, they are a species of greatest conservation need, Tier 1B, in the Arizona State Wildlife Action Plan (AGFD 2006).

BMGR-East Climate and Projections
- Annual increase in temperature 2.2 °C (4 °F) by 2050 (www.climatewizard.org, A2 emissions, ensembled GCM) and greater evaporation
- No change in average rainfall by 2050 (www.climatewizard.org, A2 emissions, ensembled GCM)
- Sonoran Desert expands northward and eastward, and contracts in the southeast (Weiss and Overpeck 2005)
- More droughts and intense storms (Seager and others 2007)
- Earlier and more intense flooding (Garfin and Lenart 2007; Seager and others 2007)
- Summer monsoon changes unknown (Mitchell and others 2002)
- Grasses favored over shrubs (Esser 1992)
- Increases in invasive grasses and fires (Esser 1992; Williams and Baruch 2000)
- CAM plants (succulents and cacti) will be resilient to increasing temperatures (Smith and others 1984)

A detailed review of projections is in the "Projections of Climate, Disturbance, and Biotic Communities" section of the main text.

Other Threats and Interactions with Climate

Based on Breeding Bird Survey data, gilded flicker populations are considered stable or possibly increasing (Moore 1995). Suitable substrates for cavity excavation are thought to be limiting in northern flickers (Moore 1995), but may be less so for gilded flickers as large cactus are softer and tend to be relatively more abundant on the landscape than large snags or trees with large dead limbs. Loss of saguaro is probably the largest threat to this species. Although cacti are well-adapted to hot, dry conditions, it may be vulnerable to fires. Cactus can survive fires, but mortality rates have been found to be higher after burning. In addition, mortality can be increased by higher fire intensities and higher frequencies, which are both induced by exotic grass invasions. Buffelgrass (Pennisetum ciliare), in particular, is a major factor in conversion of Sonoran desert habitats to grasslands. This conversion is likely to be exacerbated by climate change as more variable rainfall encourages build-up of fuels followed by dry conditions conducive to ignitions and fire spread. Even if saguaro can survive invasion and fires, seedling survival may be severely reduced (Morales-Romero and Molina-Freaner 2008). Buffelgrass may also reduce foraging success of flickers as open ground is reduced. Buffelgrass is not common on BMGR, but further introduction and spread from current locations is highly likely.

If European starling eventually expands on BMGR, it could decrease cavity availability, although one study suggests that negative impacts of starling on gilded flicker are relatively small (Kerpez and Smith 1990).

Research Needs

Other than threats related to invasive grasses, little information is available on expected response of saguaro cactus populations to climate change. Its association with a wide variety of species as well as its iconic status makes assessing threats to saguaro a high priority. Gilded flickers may also be a contributor to saguaro population dynamics as cavity excavation often results in mortality (McAuliffe and Hendricks 1988). It is unknown if climate variables such as drought or rainfall affect the rate of this mortality. Gilded flicker is less studied than the similar northern flicker. More information is needed regarding habitat requirements and quality, particularly related to foraging. Microclimate of nests may be important in a warming climate, but is poorly known in this species. Tendency to orient cavities to the north may indicate some avoidance of sun and heat (Zwartjes and Nordell 1998). Little is known about ant response to climate change, which will be critical for this species, although some preliminary research indicates numbers of ants may be lower in buffelgrass habitats (Franklin 2009).

Management Implications

Preservation of columnar cactus will be key to sustaining gilded flickers and their ecological role in the region. Management to prevent spread of buffelgrass will be critical to preserving desert landscapes with large columnar cactus in the future, so current locations should be controlled and introduction points, such as roads, should be monitored.

Habitat: Gilded flicker (*Colaptes chrysoides*)

Trait/Quality	Question	Background Info & Explanation of Score	Points
1. Area and distribution: *breeding*	Is the area or location of the associated vegetation type used for breeding activities by this species expected to change?	Lives in Sonoran desertscrub with large cactus (Moore 1995). Although Sonoran desert habitats may expand northward, no change in area is expected in this region.	0
2. Area and distribution: *non-breeding*	Is the area or location of the associated vegetation type used for non-breeding activities by this species expected to change?	Same as above.	0
3. Habitat components: *breeding*	Are specific habitat components required for breeding expected to change within associated vegetation type?	Large cactus, generally saguaro, is needed for breeding (Moore 1995). Cactus are relatively resilient to warmer temperatures (but see other threats as related to non-native grasses).	0
4. Habitat components: *non-breeding*	Are other specific habitat components required for survival during non-breeding periods expected to change within associated vegetation type?	None known.	0
5. Habitat quality	Within habitats occupied, are features of the habitat associated with better reproductive success or survival expected to change?	None known.	0
6. Ability to colonize new areas	What is the potential for this species to disperse?	Highly mobile.	-1
7. Migratory or transitional habitats	Does this species require additional habitats during migration that are separated from breeding and non-breeding habitats?	Resident species.	0

Physiology: Gilded flicker (*Colaptes chrysoides*)

Trait/Quality	Question	Background Info & Explanation of Score	Points
1. Physiological thresholds	Are limiting physiological conditions expected to change?	No data. Widespread across landscapes with a variety of conditions.	0

Physiology: Gilded flicker (*Colaptes chrysoides*)

Trait/Quality	Question	Background Info & Explanation of Score	Points
2. Sex ratio	Is sex ratio determined by temperature?	No.	0
3. Exposure to weather-related disturbance	Are disturbance events (e.g., severe storms, fires, floods) that affect survival or reproduction expected to change?	None known.	0
4. Limitations to daily activity period	Are projected temperature or precipitation regimes that influence activity period of species expected to change?	No limitations to activity known.	0
5. Survival during resource fluctuation	Does this species have flexible strategies to cope with variation in resources across multiple years?	No flexible strategies.	1
6. Metabolic rates	What is this species metabolic rate?	Moderate endothermic.	0

Phenology: Gilded flicker (*Colaptes chrysoides*)

Trait/Quality	Question	Background Info & Explanation of Score	Points
1. Cues	Does this species use temperature or moisture cues to initiate activities related to fecundity or survival (e.g., hibernation, migration, breeding)?	Not known, but breeding is likely based on a combination of internal and external cues.	0
2. Breeding timing	Are activities related to species' fecundity or survival tied to discrete resource peaks (e.g., food, breeding sites) that are expected to change?	Limited information on timing of breeding, but egg laying seems to begin in early April (Moore 1995). No information on potential resource peaks or other variables related to breeding timing.	0
3. Mismatch potential	What is the separation in time or space between cues that initiate activities related to survival or fecundity and discrete events that provide critical resources?	No large separation in timing, but also does not adjust breeding directly to resource timing.	0
4. Resilience to timing mismatches during breeding	Is reproduction in this species more likely to co-occur with important events?	Only one brood per season (Moore 1995).	1

Biotic Interactions: Gilded flicker (*Colaptes chrysoides*)			
Trait/Quality	**Question**	**Background Info & Explanation of Score**	**Points**
1. Food resources	Are important food resources for this species expected to change?	Not closely studied in this species, but red-shafted flicker eats mostly ants (Moore 1995). Probably eats other ground insects as well as some seeds and fruits (Moore 1995). No studies are available, but overall reduction in ants is not expected.	0
2. Predators	Are important predator populations expected to change?	Limited information, but small raptors have been observed depredating flickers. Nestlings are protected to some extent in cavities, although still vulnerable to snake and rodent predation. No strong response to nest predators observed in adults (Moore 1995).	0
3. Symbionts	Are populations of symbiotic species expected to change?	No symbionts, although many other species depend on the cavities it excavates.	0
4. Disease	Is prevalence of diseases known to cause widespread mortality or reproductive failure in this species expected to change?	None known.	0
5. Competitors	Are populations of important competing species expected to change?	Sometimes hybridizes with red-shafted flicker, but usually only in riparian areas (Moore 1995). May compete with European starlings for cavities (Moore 1995), but starlings are currently uncommon at BMGR.	0

Literature Cited

Arizona Game and Fish Department. 2006. DRAFT. Arizona's Comprehensive Wildlife Conservation Strategy: 2005-2015. Arizona Game and Fish Department, Phoenix, AZ.

Bagne, K. E., M. M. Friggens, and D. M. Finch. 2011. A system for assessing vulnerability of species (SAVS) to climate change. USDA Forest Service, Rocky Mountain Research Station, Gen. Tech. Rep. RMRS-GTR-257.

Esser, G. 1992. Implications of climate change for production and decomposition in grasslands and coniferous forests. Ecological Applications 2:47-54.

Franklin, K. 2009. The consequences of buffelgrass pasture development for biodiversity in the southern Sonoran Desert. Dissertation, University of Arizona, AZ.

Garfin, G. and M. Lenart. 2007. Climate change effects on Southwest water resources. Southwest Hydrology 6:16-17.

Hall, J. A., P. Comer, A. Gondor, R. Marshall, and S. Weinstein. 2001. Conservation Elements of and a Biodiversity Management Framework for the Barry M. Goldwater Range, Arizona. The Nature Conservancy of Arizona, Tucson.

Kerpez, T. A. and N. S. Smith. 1990. Competition between European starlings and native woodpeckers for nest cavities in saguaros. Auk 107:367-375.

McAuliffe, J. R. and P. Hendricks. 1988. Determinants of the vertical distributions of woodpecker nest cavities in the Sahuaro cactus. The Condor 90:791-801.

Mitchell, D. L., D. Ivanova, R. Rabin, K. Redmond, and T. J. Brown. 2002. Gulf of California sea surface temperatures and the North American monsoon: mechanistic implications from observations. Journal of Climate 15:2261-2281.

Moore, W. S. 1995. Gilded Flicker (*Colaptes chrysoides*). In A. Poole. ed., The Birds of North America Online. Ithaca: Cornell Lab of Ornithology.

Morales-Romero, D. and F. Molina-Freaner. 2008. Influence of buffelgrass pasture conversion on the regeneration and reproduction of the columnar cactus, *Pachycereus pecten-aboriginum*, in northwestern Mexico. Journal of Arid Environments 72:228-237.

Seager, R., T. Mingfang, I. Held, [and others]. 2007. Model projections of an imminent transition to a more arid climate in southwestern North America. Science 316:1181-1184.

Smith, S. D., B. Didden-Zopfy, and P. S. Nobel. 1984. High-temperature responses of North American cacti. Ecology 65:643-651.

Weiss, J. L. and J. T. Overpeck. 2005. Is the Sonoran Desert losing its cool? Global Change Biology 11:2065-2077.

Williams, D. G., and Z. Baruch. 2000. African grass invasion in the Americas: ecosystem consequences and the role of ecophysiology. Biological Invasions 2:213-140.

Zwartjes, P. W. and S. E. Nordell. 1998. Patterns of cavity-entrance orientation by gilded flickers (*Colaptes chrysoides*) in Cardón cactus. The Auk 115: 119-126.

Le Conte's Thrasher
(*Toxostoma lecontei*)

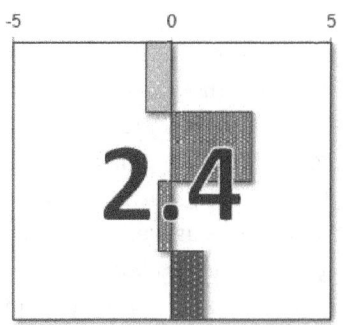

SUMMARY

Le Conte's thrasher occupies sparsely vegetated desert washes and dunes subject to very high temperatures. The species is well adapted to these conditions and is likely to be resilient to future climate change based on many features of its biology, but with climate becoming even more extreme, this species could experience population declines associated with physiological limitations.

VULNERABILITY	Score	Uncertainty
Habitat	**-0.8**	14%
Physiology	**2.5**	50%
Phenology	**-0.4**	50%
Interactions	**1.0**	40%
Overall	**2.4**	**36%**

Figure Key

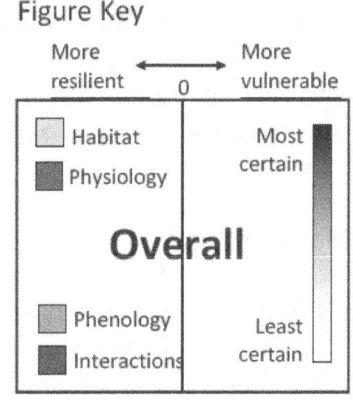

Introduction

Le Conte's thrasher is associated with extremely dry habitats in the southwestern United States extending into parts of Mexico. It is a Federal species of concern and a species of greatest conservation need, Tier 1B, from the Arizona State Wildlife Action Plan (AGFD 2006).

BMGR-East Climate and Projections

- Annual increase in temperature 2.2 °C (4 °F) by 2050 (www.climatewizard.org, A2 emissions, ensembled GCM) and greater evaporation
- No change in average rainfall by 2050 (www.climatewizard.org, A2 emissions, ensembled GCM)
- Sonoran Desert expands northward and eastward, and contracts in the southeast (Weiss and Overpeck 2005)
- More droughts and intense storms (Seager and others 2007)
- Earlier and more intense flooding (Garfin and Lenart 2007; Seager and others 2007)
- Summer monsoon changes unknown (Mitchell and others 2002)
- Grasses favored over shrubs (Esser 1992)
- Increases in invasive grasses and fires (Esser 1992; Williams and Baruch 2000)

A detailed review of projections is in the "Projections of Climate, Disturbance, and Biotic Communities" section of the main text.

Other Threats and Interactions with Climate

Major population reductions have mostly been from loss of habitat due to development (Sheppard 1996). Off-highway vehicle or other traffic, which can concentrate in washes and sparse vegetation, may degrade habitats. Vehicular traffic may increase with climate change. Buffering of climate impacts varies with factors such as irrigation and government programs, both of which predict that drought impacts will be less severe in the United States as compared to Mexico (Vásquez-León and others 2003). In the absence of alterations to immigration policies, increased illegal traffic at the international border is expected. Threats on BMGR identified by Arizona Game and Fish Department include ground-based training and heavy equipment maneuvers as well as invasive plant species such as Sahara mustard (*Brassica tournefortii*) and Mediterranean grass (*Schismus barbatus*). Spread of invasive plants is particularly concerning as they can enhance the spread of fire through sparsely vegetated lands, which can contribute to degradation of thrasher habitats (Brown and Minnich 1986). Climate change is likely to exacerbate spread of these invasive plants and increases in fires, in part, through more variable rainfall that results in very wet years followed by very dry years that are conducive to large fires.

Research Needs

The breeding bird survey rarely detects Le Conte's thrasher because surveys occur after most singing has ended (Sheppard 1996). Thus, population trends are unknown in this species. Although well adapted to desert conditions, there is no information on the species about the effects of droughts or flooding, both of which may increase in frequency and/or severity. In addition, competitive interactions with other thrashers and relation to habitat variables are not well known but are important for considering future population trajectories.

Management Implications

BMGR has few of the known major threats to this species. Management planning should include the expectation of increasing threats from vehicles and border security activities. This species generally does not occur near water or in areas where other thrasher species dominate. Activities that increase suitability for other thrasher species, such as encouraging shrub growth or installing water features, could be detrimental to Le Conte's thrasher. Conversely, some areas may increase in suitability as hotter and drier conditions decrease shrub cover in areas where cover is currently too high to attract this species. Monitoring designed to detect this species may be warranted in locations with potential impacts. Finally, activity restrictions to avoid breeding disturbance should anticipate potential changes in breeding timing.

Habitat: Le Conte's thrasher (*Toxostoma lecontei*)			
Trait/Quality	**Question**	**Background Info & Explanation of Score**	**Points**
1. Area and distribution: *breeding*	Is the area or location of the associated vegetation type used for breeding activities by this species expected to change?	Occurs in sparsely vegetated desert shrublands and dunes with low relief topography and sandy soils (Sheppard 1996). Often associated with salt bush, cholla, and creosote. Areas with greater shrub cover are generally occupied by other thrasher species (Sheppard 1996). Although areas of sparse vegetation may increase, suitable soil and topography will not. Overall area is not expected to change.	0
2. Area and distribution: *non-breeding*	Is the area or location of the associated vegetation type used for non-breeding activities by this species expected to change?	Same as above.	0
3. Habitat components: *breeding*	Are specific habitat components required for breeding expected to change within associated vegetation type?	Nests often in saltbush or cholla cactus. Young may disperse 1-3 km from the nest (Sheppard 1996). Cholla cactus and saltbush likely not reduced.	0
4. Habitat components: *non-breeding*	Are other specific habitat components required for survival during non-breeding periods expected to change within associated vegetation type?	Availability of secure night roosts likely important (Sheppard 1996). Roosts and nests in shrubs with dense foliage or thorny cactus, occasionally in small trees such as smoke tree (Sheppard 1996).	0
5. Habitat quality	Within habitats occupied, are features of the habitat associated with better reproductive success or survival expected to change?	Feeds in litter under desert shrubs, but no known variable associated with better foraging success. It is also not associated with dense shrub cover, but this may be because of competitive interactions.	0
6. Ability to colonize new areas	What is the potential for this species to disperse?	Highly mobile.	-1
7. Migratory or transitional habitats	Does this species require additional habitats during migration that are separated from breeding and non-breeding habitats?	Not migratory.	0

Physiology: Le Conte's thrasher (*Toxostoma lecontei*)			
Trait/Quality	**Question**	**Background Info & Explanation of Score**	**Points**
1. Physiological thresholds	Are limiting physiological conditions expected to change?	Can endure extremely hot surface temperatures (Sheppard 1996). BMGR habitats it occupies are already very hot. Although well adapted to current conditions, this species will be exposed to higher temperatures with little means of escape. May not tolerate further increases.	1
2. Sex ratio	Is sex ratio determined by temperature?	No.	0
3. Exposure to weather-related disturbance	Are disturbance events (e.g., severe storms, fires, floods) that affect survival or reproduction expected to change?	Few nests lost during cold and rainy weather in California (Sheppard 1996).	0
4. Limitations to daily activity period	Are projected temperature or precipitation regimes that influence activity period of species expected to change?	Generally inactive during very high temperatures. Limits activities during hottest part of the day, thus these periods may increase.	1
5. Survival during resource fluctuation	Does this species have flexible strategies to cope with variation in resources across multiple years?	None known.	1
6. Metabolic rates	What is this species metabolic rate?	Moderate endothermic.	0

Phenology: Le Conte's thrasher (*Toxostoma lecontei*)			
Trait/Quality	**Question**	**Background Info & Explanation of Score**	**Points**
1. Cues	Does this species use temperature or moisture cues to initiate activities related to fecundity or survival (e.g., hibernation, migration, breeding)?	Not known, but likely a combination of internal and external signals.	0
2. Breeding timing	Are activities related to species' fecundity or survival tied to discrete resource peaks (e.g., food, breeding sites) that are expected to change?	No evidence of breeding following summer monsoons. Probably begin egg laying in mid-February in Arizona (Sheppard 1996) with breeding activities ceasing by June. Timing may relate to cooler temperatures for vulnerable young in the nest, thus changes are expected.	1

Phenology: Le Conte's thrasher (*Toxostoma lecontei*)

Trait/Quality	Question	Background Info & Explanation of Score	Points
3. Mismatch potential	What is the separation in time or space between cues that initiate activities related to survival or fecundity and discrete events that provide critical resources?	Activities are not distant from cues.	0
4. Resilience to timing mismatches during breeding	Is reproduction in this species more likely to co-occur with important events?	Often have two broods per year (Sheppard 1996).	-1

Biotic Interactions: Le Conte's thrasher (*Toxostoma lecontei*)

Trait/Quality	Question	Background Info & Explanation of Score	Points
1. Food resources	Are important food resources for this species expected to change?	Eats mostly arthropods, although bird eggs, small lizards, and seeds may also be eaten. Digs for arthropods in litter and sandy soils. Arthropods occupying litter may be reduced with drier conditions.	1
2. Predators	Are important predator populations expected to change?	Various predators on nests and one report of an adult eaten by a prairie falcon (Sheppard 1996). Predation is not likely a major factor in mortality.	0
3. Symbionts	Are populations of symbiotic species expected to change?	No symbionts.	0
4. Disease	Is prevalence of diseases known to cause widespread mortality or reproductive failure in this species expected to change?	No major diseases known.	0
5. Competitors	Are populations of important competing species expected to change?	May compete with other thrashers for habitat and other birds for nesting sites, but no known effect on populations. It is possible that this species' adaptations to extreme conditions will allow it to compete better than other thrashers in a warming climate, but no available information on competitive interactions.	0

Literature Cited

Arizona Game and Fish Department. 2006. DRAFT. Arizona's Comprehensive Wildlife Conservation Strategy: 2005-2015. Arizona Game and Fish Department, Phoenix, AZ.

Bagne, K. E., M. M. Friggens, and D. M. Finch. 2011. A system for assessing vulnerability of species (SAVS) to climate change. USDA Forest Service, Rocky Mountain Research Station, Gen. Tech. Rep. RMRS-GTR-257.

Brown, D. E., and R. A. Minnich. 1986. Fire and changes in creosote bush scrub of the western Sonoran Desert, California. American Midland Naturalist 116:411-422.

Esser, G. 1992. Implications of climate change for production and decomposition in grasslands and coniferous forests. Ecological Applications 2:47-54.

Garfin, G. and M. Lenart. 2007. Climate change effects on Southwest water resources. Southwest Hydrology 6:16-17.

Mitchell, D. L., D. Ivanova, R. Rabin, K. Redmond, and T. J. Brown. 2002. Gulf of California sea surface temperatures and the North American monsoon: mechanistic implications from observations. Journal of Climate 15:2261-2281.

Seager, R., T. Ming, I. Held, [and others]. 2007. Model projections of an imminent transition to a more arid climate in southwestern North America. Science 316:1181-1184.

Sheppard, J. M. 1996. Le Conte's Thrasher (*Toxostoma lecontei*). In A. Poole, ed., The Birds of North America Online. Ithaca: Cornell Lab of Ornithology.

Vásquez-León, M., C. T. West, and T. J. Finan. 2003. A comparative assessment of climate vulnerability: agriculture and ranching on both sides of the US-Mexico border. Global Environmental Change 13:159-173.

Weiss, J. L. and J. T. Overpeck. 2005. Is the Sonoran Desert losing its cool? Global Change Biology 11:2065-2077.

Williams, D. G. and Z. Baruch. 2000. African grass invasion in the Americas: ecosystem consequences and the role of ecophysiology. Biological Invasions 2:213-140.

Cave Myotis
(*Myotis velifer*)

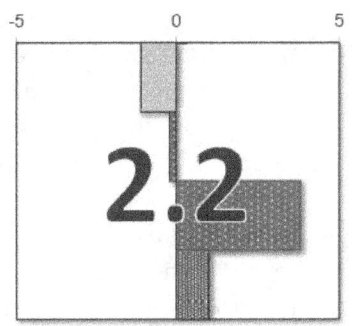

SUMMARY

Vulnerability of the cave myotis to population declines is increased under climate change projections. This species both migrates and hibernates, two activities associated with timing changes that may lead to mis-matches with other events such as insect emergence or suitable breeding conditions. Timing relationships are complex, thus eventual outcome in the future is unknown and periodic monitoring is recommended. Roosts and open water sources are important elements for this species and should be considered in management planning.

VULNERABILITY	Score	Uncertainty
Habitat	**-1.1**	14%
Physiology	**-0.2**	33%
Phenology	**3.8**	25%
Interactions	**1.0**	60%
Overall	**2.2**	**32%**

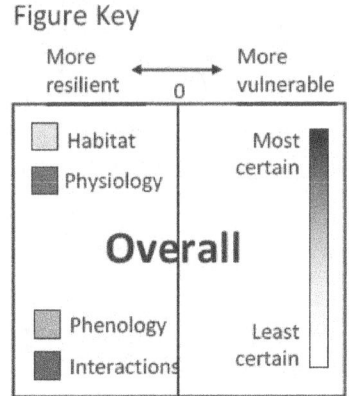

Figure Key

Introduction
The cave myotis occurs on BMGR. It has been a Federal species of concern since 1994. The U.S. Forest Service also identifies it as sensitive. Despite being widespread, this species is threatened locally, particularly in western portions of its range.

BMGR-East Climate and Projections
- Annual increase in temperature 2.2 °C (4 °F) by 2050 (www.climatewizard.org, A2 emissions, ensembled GCM) and greater evaporation
- No change in average rainfall by 2050 (www.climatewizard.org, A2 emissions, ensembled GCM)
- Sonoran Desert expands northward and eastward, and contracts in the southeast (Weiss and Overpeck 2005)
- More droughts and intense storms (Seager and others 2007)
- Earlier and more intense flooding (Garfin and Lenart 2007; Seager and others 2007)
- Summer monsoon changes unknown (Mitchell and others 2002)
- Grasses favored over shrubs (Esser 1992)
- Increases in invasive grasses and fires (Esser 1992; Williams and Baruch 2000)
- Warmer temperatures and decreased soil moisture in Mexico (Liverman and O'Brien 1991)

A detailed review of projections is in the "Projections of Climate, Disturbance, and Biotic Communities" section of the main text.

Other Threats and Interactions with Climate

The patchy distribution of this species may be due to its reliance on caves. Recent population declines in cave myotis are thought to be related to local habitat loss (BISON-M). Cave myotis, like many other bats, is vulnerable to disturbance at roosts, especially at maternity roosts.

Research Needs

More information on suitable roost sites at a local level is needed as this feature affects species presence. Threat of white-nosed fungus for Arizona bats will be important to the species overall, but this disease may have limited effects on BMGR. More information is needed to understand the threat of this disease in areas outside its known range. Importance of various foraging habitats is not well known. How populations may be affected by drought conditions will be critical to predicting climate change effects.

Management Implications

Most cave myotis winter outside of Arizona, and their affinity for cool, moist hibernacula is unlikely to increase winter presence in the future. Maternity roost on the other hand may become more critical and suitability may be altered over time. Potential roost sites should be checked periodically for species presence. Any restrictions that span specific dates intended to protect bats should anticipate changes in timing of bat activities. Some monitoring of populations is warranted, as identified phenological vulnerability will have an uncertain outcome on populations because interactions with resources are more complex than can be evaluated here. Flexibility in migratory behaviors will likely help this species cope with changes on a broad scale, but will increase the likelihood of population changes on BMGR and other parts of Arizona.

Habitat: Cave myotis (*Myotis velifer*)			
Trait/Quality	**Question**	**Background Info & Explanation of Score**	**Points**
1. Area and distribution: *breeding*	Is the area or location of the associated vegetation type used for breeding activities by this species expected to change?	Occurs in various desert grassland habitats, but also been found in pinyon-juniper woodland (BISON-M). Grasslands may increase with warmer temperatures.	-1
2. Area and distribution: *non-breeding*	Is the area or location of the associated vegetation type used for non-breeding activities by this species expected to change?	May move to southwestern Mexico for winter (BISON-M). Assume similar habitats to breeding.	-1
3. Habitat components: *breeding*	Are specific habitat components required for breeding expected to change within associated vegetation type?	Roosts in caves and mines, occasionally buildings or bridges. Often found near the entrance (BISON-M). Caves and mines will not change with climate.	0
4. Habitat components: *non-breeding*	Are other specific habitat components required for survival during non-breeding periods expected to change within associated vegetation type?	Prefers moist caves for hibernation (NatureServe 2009). In Arizona, winter roosts are in moist caves above 6000 ft. Cave availability is not expected to change (but see Physiology, Question 1).	0
5. Habitat quality	Within habitats occupied, are features of the habitat associated with better reproductive success or survival expected to change?	In Arizona, often in vicinity of water sources (Hoffmeister 1986). It is likely that these features are important for successful foraging and likely to decline with warmer temperatures.	1
6. Ability to colonize new areas	What is the potential for this species to disperse?	Highly mobile.	-1
7. Migratory or transitional habitats	Does this species require additional habitats during migration that are separated from breeding and non-breeding habitats?	Mostly migratory in Arizona although migratory behavior seems somewhat flexible (NatureServe 2009).	1

Physiology: Cave myotis (*Myotis velifer*)

Trait/Quality	Question	Background Info & Explanation of Score	Points
1. Physiological thresholds	Are limiting physiological conditions expected to change?	Ranges from the southwestern and central United States into Central America. Preferred hibernaculum temperature is 8 to 9° C (Hoffmeister 1986). Most bats in Arizona migrate to hibernate, but those that remain seek out moist, cool habitats (Hoffmeister 1986). Not known if warmer, drier conditions will exceed thresholds, but they may. Rely on moist, cool caves for hibernation, which will warm and lose moisture with increasing temperatures.	1
2. Sex ratio	Is sex ratio determined by temperature?	No.	0
3. Exposure to weather-related disturbance	Are disturbance events (e.g., severe storms, fires, floods) that affect survival or reproduction expected to change?	None known. Buffered from extremes, to some extent, in hibernaculum.	0
4. Limitations to daily activity period	Are projected temperature or precipitation regimes that influence activity period of species expected to change?	Nocturnal. No expected changes in activity.	0
5. Survival during resource fluctuation	Does this species have flexible strategies to cope with variation in resources across multiple years?	Sperm is stored over winter, which may maintain breeding with population and resource fluctuations. In addition, migratory behavior may be flexible (NatureServe 2009)	-1
6. Metabolic rates	What is this species metabolic rate?	Moderate endothermic.	0

Phenology: Cave myotis (*Myotis velifer*)

Trait/Quality	Question	Background Info & Explanation of Score	Points
1. Cues	Does this species use temperature or moisture cues to initiate activities related to fecundity or survival (e.g., hibernation, migration, breeding)?	Emergence from roosts is later after sunset in summer than spring (NatureServe 2009) and is apparently signaled by exterior light levels (Hoffmeister 1986). Other cues not known.	0
2. Breeding timing	Are activities related to species' fecundity or survival tied to discrete resource peaks (e.g., food, breeding sites) that are expected to change?	Young born mid to late June in Arizona, and females leave maternity colonies in August (NatureServe 2009). Favorable weather conditions and insect peaks are likely to change timing.	1

Phenology: Cave myotis (*Myotis velifer*)

Trait/Quality	Question	Background Info & Explanation of Score	Points
3. Mismatch potential	What is the separation in time or space between cues that initiate activities related to survival or fecundity and discrete events that provide critical resources?	Bats in Mexico moved to higher-elevation caves to hibernate (NatureServe 2009), perhaps to take advantage of colder conditions. Emergence from hibernation and migration occurs far from insect emergence and feeding of young.	1
4. Resilience to timing mismatches during breeding	Is reproduction in this species more likely to co-occur with important events?	One reproductive event per year.	1

Biotic Interactions: Cave myotis (*Myotis velifer*)

Trait/Quality	Question	Background Info & Explanation of Score	Points
1. Food resources	Are important food resources for this species expected to change?	Insectivorous and likely opportunistic (NatureServe 2009). Overall, prey levels not expected to change.	0
2. Predators	Are important predator populations expected to change?	Likely various. No overall changes in predation expected.	0
3. Symbionts	Are populations of symbiotic species expected to change?	Hibernates in large clusters and occupies roosts with other species (NatureServe 2009). May have thermal advantages, but no known changes in clusters.	0
4. Disease	Is prevalence of diseases known to cause widespread mortality or reproductive failure in this species expected to change?	Single bat found in May 2010 with white-nose syndrome from western Oklahoma was from this species (USFWS news release: 19 May 2010). This is the first reported occurrence of the disease in this species and the first from west of the Mississippi, although no associated mortality was reported. Transmission may increase if individuals are restricted to fewer suitable roosts.	1
5. Competitors	Are populations of important competing species expected to change?	*Myotis lucifugus occultus* may exclude this species from suitable habitat (BISON-M). No known changes in this species although likely to be similarly vulnerable.	0

Literature Cited

Bagne, K. E., M. M. Friggens, and D. M. Finch. 2011. A system for assessing vulnerability of species (SAVS) to climate change. USDA Forest Service, Rocky Mountain Research Station, Gen. Tech. Rep. RMRS-GTR-257.

BISON-M. Biotic Information System of New Mexico [web application]. New Mexico Game and Fish Department. Online at: http://www.bison-m.org.

Esser, G. 1992. Implications of climate change for production and decomposition in grasslands and coniferous forests. Ecological Applications 2:47-54.

Garfin, G. and M. Lenart. 2007. Climate change effects on Southwest water resources. Southwest Hydrology 6:16-17.

Liverman, D. M. and K. L. O'Brien. 1991. Global warming and climate change in Mexico. Pages 351-364 In Global Environmental Change. Butterworth-Heinemann Ltd.

Hoffmeister, D. F. 1986. Mammals of Arizona. University of Arizona Press and Arizona Game and Fish Dept. 602 p.

Mitchell, D. L., D. Ivanova, R. Rabin, K. Redmond, and T. J. Brown. 2002. Gulf of California sea surface temperatures and the North American monsoon: mechanistic implications from observations. Journal of Climate 15:2261-2281.

NatureServe. 2009. NatureServe Explorer: an online encyclopedia of life [web application]. Version 7.1. NatureServe, Arlington, Virginia. Online at: http://www.natureserve.org/explorer. (Accessed: December 2, 2009)

Seager, R., T. Mingfang, I. Held, [and others]. 2007. Model projections of an imminent transition to a more arid climate in southwestern North America. Science 316:1181-1184.

Weiss, J. L. and J. T. Overpeck. 2005. Is the Sonoran Desert losing its cool? Global Change Biology 11:2065-2077.

Williams, D. G. and Z. Baruch. 2000. African grass invasion in the Americas: ecosystem consequences and the role of ecophysiology. Biological Invasions 2:213-140.

California Leaf-nosed Bat
(*Macrotus californicus*)

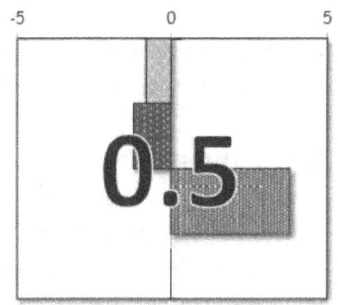

SUMMARY

Overall, California leaf-nosed bats are not expected to be vulnerable to climate-related population declines. Phenology, however, is related to a number of predicted changes that could be detrimental to this species. Considerable uncertainty surrounds threats related to timing changes, for which the ultimate outcome of the population is unknown. Periodic monitoring of populations, including assessment of potential roosts, is recommended.

VULNERABILITY	Score	Uncertainty
Habitat	**-0.8**	14%
Physiology	**-1.2**	33%
Phenology	**3.8**	50%
Interactions	**0.0**	60%
Overall	**0.5**	**36%**

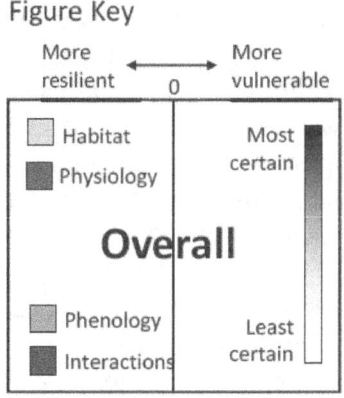

Introduction

The scientific name has been revised from *Macrotus waterhousii californicus*. California leaf-nosed bat occurs in the Sonoran Desert of North America and is unusual for the inclusion of cactus fruit in its diet and for remaining active throughout the year. In addition, it does not migrate. This is the most common bat species on BMGR and 11 active roost sites are known (Hall and others 2001). Individuals can have large home ranges, and foraging habitat may include BMGR as well as surrounding lands (Dalton 2001). The California leaf-nosed bat is a Federal species of concern. It is listed by the Bureau of Land Management as sensitive and by Arizona Game and Fish Department as a species of greatest conservation need (AGFD 2006). In addition, this species was ranked by the Western Bat Working Group as at a high risk of imperilment and is a conservation element for the proposed biodiversity management framework (Hall and others 2001).

BMGR-East Climate and Projections

- Annual increase in temperature 2.2 °C (4 °F) by 2050 (www.climatewizard.org, A2 emissions, ensembled GCM) and greater evaporation
- No change in average rainfall by 2050 (www.climatewizard.org, A2 emissions, ensembled GCM)
- Sonoran Desert expands northward and eastward, and contracts in the southeast (Weiss and Overpeck 2005)
- More droughts and intense storms (Seager and others 2007)
- Earlier and more intense flooding (Garfin and Lenart 2007; Seager and others 2007)
- Summer monsoon changes unknown (Mitchell and others 2002)
- Grasses favored over shrubs (Esser 1992)
- Increases in invasive grasses and fires (Esser 1992; Williams and Baruch 2000)

A detailed review of projections is in the "Projections of Climate, Disturbance, and Biotic Communities" section of the main text.

Other Threats and Interactions with Climate

Disturbance at roosts is an important threat to bat species. Pesticide use threatens insect prey (Hall and others 2001), but is unlikely to increase with climate change. Disturbance at roosts may be expected to increase in some regions along the United States-Mexico border with negative impacts on roosting bats. Increased droughts predicted under future climate scenarios will result in failure of agricultural crops and will put stress on growing human populations. Buffering of climate impacts varies with factors such as irrigation and government programs, both of which predict that drought impacts will be less severe in the United States as compared to Mexico (Vásquez-León and others 2003). In the absence of alterations to immigration policies, increased illegal traffic at the international border is expected and, subsequently, an increase in human use of caves and disturbance at roosts.

Research Needs

The Biodiversity Management Framework for BMGR (Hall and others 2001) notes several research needs for California leaf-nosed bat: What are its water requirements and how is it affected by artificial waters? How is it affected by variation in rainfall? In addition, because its range is thought to be limited by the availability of warm roosts, we also question if there are potential roosts that will become suitable with warmer conditions at BMGR and surrounding lands. Habitat quality can be important for maintaining populations, but we found no information linking habitat to reproduction or survival. This type of research could suggest strategies for successful management of populations.

Management Implications

Although abandoned mines and caves are not expected to be threatened by climate change, their protection will remain critical to overall management. In addition, warmer winter temperatures may change suitability of roost sites, thus unoccupied sites cannot be assumed to remain so. Potential roost sites should be checked periodically for species presence. Some monitoring of populations is warranted, as their identified phenological vulnerability will have an uncertain outcome on populations because interactions with resources are more complex than can be evaluated here. Although this species will be subject to changes in timing, it may prove to be adaptable. Any restrictions that span specific dates intended to protect bats should anticipate changes in timing of bat activities.

Habitat: California leaf-nosed bat (*Macrotus californicus*)

Trait/Quality	Question	Background Info & Explanation of Score	Points
1. Area and distribution: *breeding*	Is the area or location of the associated vegetation type used for breeding activities by this species expected to change?	The California leaf-nosed bat lives in various desert scrub habitats of the Sonoran desert. Xeroriparian areas may be particularly important for foraging (Hall and others 2001). Sonoran desert habitats are expected to expand northward in the United States, but BMGR is likely to remain the same general vegetation type and area.	0
2. Area and distribution: *non-breeding*	Is the area or location of the associated vegetation type used for non-breeding activities by this species expected to change?	Same as above.	0
3. Habitat components: *breeding*	Are specific habitat components required for breeding expected to change within associated vegetation type?	It uses caves and old mines for day and maternity roosts (NatureServe 2009), as well as bridges, porches, culverts, caves and other structures to rest at night while foraging. Needs caves or old mines for maternity roosts. Availability not expected to change.	0
4. Habitat components: *non-breeding*	Are other specific habitat components required for survival during non-breeding periods expected to change within associated vegetation type?	Needs caves or old mines for day roosts. Also uses various crevices for night roosts. Availability not expected to change.	0
5. Habitat quality	Within habitats occupied, are features of the habitat associated with better reproductive success or survival expected to change?	No known habitat associations with increased reproduction.	0
6. Ability to colonize new areas	What is the potential for this species to disperse?	Highly mobile.	-1
7. Migratory or transitional habitats	Does this species require additional habitats during migration that are separated from breeding and non-breeding habitats?	Not migratory.	0

Physiology: California leaf-nosed bat (*Macrotus californicus*)

Trait/Quality	Question	Background Info & Explanation of Score	Points
1. Physiological thresholds	Are limiting physiological conditions expected to change?	The leaf-nosed bat is intolerant of cold temperatures, and although it does not hibernate (NatureServe 2009), it depends on roosts to escape cold temperatures. Roosts can also be used to escape hot conditions. Thermal neutral zone is 33 °C to 40 °C. Warmer winter temperatures may improve survival.	-1
2. Sex ratio	Is sex ratio determined by temperature?	No.	0
3. Exposure to weather-related disturbance	Are disturbance events (e.g., severe storms, fires, floods) that affect survival or reproduction expected to change?	Behaviors adapted to desert conditions include roosting in warm conditions in winter. Exposure to cold temperatures can cause death. No other information.	-1
4. Limitations to daily activity period	Are projected temperature or precipitation regimes that influence activity period of species expected to change?	Mostly active around sunrise and sunset. Intolerant of cold temperatures and roosts during the day, avoiding the warmest temperatures. Activity period expected to remain approximately the same (but see Question 1).	0
5. Survival during resource fluctuation	Does this species have flexible strategies to cope with variation in resources across multiple years?	No. It is thought that the species is probably able to tolerate desert conditions because of foraging and roosting behavior rather than specialized physiology (Bell and others 1986), but there is no recent research on this topic.	1
6. Metabolic rates	What is this species metabolic rate?	Moderate endothermic.	0

Phenology: California leaf-nosed bat (*Macrotus californicus*)

Trait/Quality	Question	Background Info & Explanation of Score	Points
1. Cues	Does this species use temperature or moisture cues to initiate activities related to fecundity or survival (e.g., hibernation, migration, breeding)?	Mating takes place in the fall and young are born in May and June (NatureServe 2009). This long gestation period is sustained by delayed embryonic development. Embryonic development is slow during winter then speeds up. No known relation of cues to temperature.	0
2. Breeding timing	Are activities related to species' fecundity or survival tied to discrete resource peaks (e.g., food, breeding sites) that are expected to change?	Young are born in the spring, likely corresponding to favorable temperatures and/or emergence of insects. Emergence of moths and cicadas is related to temperature and prone to timing change.	1
3. Mismatch potential	What is the separation in time or space between cues that initiate activities related to survival or	Mating occurs far in advance of birth of young. The trigger or mechanism behind this increase in development rate could be temperature related.	1

Phenology: California leaf-nosed bat (*Macrotus californicus*)			
Trait/Quality	**Question**	**Background Info & Explanation of Score**	**Points**
	fecundity and discrete events that provide critical resources?		
4. Resilience to timing mismatches during breeding	Is reproduction in this species more likely to co-occur with important events?	One reproductive event per year.	1

Biotic Interactions: California leaf-nosed bat (*Macrotus californicus*)			
Trait/Quality	**Question**	**Background Info & Explanation of Score**	**Points**
1. Food resources	Are important food resources for this species expected to change?	Primary prey are flying insects that are active at night such as moths, beetles, and grasshoppers (NatureServe 2009). No projections known related to changes in nocturnal insects. Cicadas are taken and are resilient to high temperatures (Heath and others 1970). Occasionally, leaf-nosed bats also feed on cactus fruits. Foraging may be concentrated around xeroriparian corridors, areas with high densities of saguaro cactus, and tinajas (Hall and others 2001). Unknown changes in abundance of prey.	0
2. Predators	Are important predator populations expected to change?	Probably various, but no specific information.	0
3. Symbionts	Are populations of symbiotic species expected to change?	No symbionts. California leaf-nosed bats will roost with other bat species, but also in single species aggregates (Arita 1993).	0
4. Disease	Is prevalence of diseases known to cause widespread mortality or reproductive failure in this species expected to change?	Species is susceptible to rabies. Rabies can result in mortality, but is generally not considered a threat to bat colonies (Gillette and Kimbrough 1970). Another emerging bat disease is white-nose syndrome, which has been killing large numbers of roosting bats in northeastern North America. So far, it appears this disease only threatens hibernating species and is associated with cold conditions (Blehert and others 2008). California leaf-nosed bats have neither of these risk factors.	0
5. Competitors	Are populations of important competing species expected to change?	No known competitors.	0

Literature Cited

Arizona Game and Fish Department. 2006. DRAFT. Arizona's Comprehensive Wildlife Conservation Strategy: 2005-2015. Arizona Game and Fish Department, Phoenix, AZ.

Arita, H. T. 1993. Conservation biology of the cave bats of Mexico. Journal of Mammalogy 74:693-702.

Bagne, K. E., M. M. Friggens, and D. M. Finch. 2011. A system for assessing vulnerability of species (SAVS) to climate change. USDA Forest Service, Rocky Mountain Research Station, Gen. Tech. Rep. RMRS-GTR-257.

Bell, G. P., G. A. Bartholomew, and K. A. Nagy. 1986. The roles of energetics, water economy, foraging behavior, and geothermal refugia in the distribution of the bat, *Macrotus californicus*. Journal of Comparative Physiology 156:441-450.

Cockrum, E. L. and S. P. Cross. 1964. Time of bat activity over water holes. Journal of Mammalogy 45:635-636.

Environment and Natural Resources Division. December 2006. Programmic Biological Assessment for Ongoing and Future Military Operations and Activities at Fort Huachuca, Arizona.

Garfin, G. and M. Lenart. 2007. Climate change effects on Southwest water resources. Southwest Hydrology 6:16-17.

Gillette, D. D. and J. D. Kimbrough. 1970. Chiropteran Mortality. In B. Slaugher and D. Walton, eds. About Bats. Southern Methodist University Press, Dallas, TX.

Hall, J. A., P. Comer, A. Gondor, R. Marshall, and S. Weinstein. 2001. Conservation Elements of and a Biodiversity Management Framework for the Barry M. Goldwater Range, Arizona. The Nature Conservancy of Arizona, Tucson.

Heath, J. E. and P. J. Wilkin. 1970. Temperature responses of the desert cicada, *Diceroprocta apache* (Homoptera, Cicadidae). Physiological Zoology 43:145-154.

McLaughlin, S. E. and J. P. Bowers. 1982. Effects of wildfire on a Sonoran Desert plant community. Ecology 63:246-248.

Mitchell, D. L., D. Ivanova, R. Rabin, K. Redmond, and T. J. Brown. 2002. Gulf of California sea surface temperatures and the North American monsoon: Mechanistic implications from observations. Journal of Climate 15:2261-2281.

NatureServe. 2009. NatureServe Explorer: an online encyclopedia of life [web application]. Version 7.1. NatureServe, Arlington, Virginia. Online at: http://www.natureserve.org/explorer. (Accessed: December 2, 2009)

Pinkava, D. J. 1999. Cactaceae cactus family, part three, Cylindropuntia. Journal of the Arizona-Nevada Academy of Science 32:32-47.

Seager, R., T. Ming, I. Held, [and others]. 2007. Model projections of an imminent transition to a more arid climate in southwestern North America. Science 316:1181-1184.

Vásquez-León, M., C. T. West, and T. J. Finan. 2003. A comparative assessment of climate vulnerability: agriculture and ranching on both sides of the US-Mexico border. Global Environmental Change 13:159-173.

Weiss, J. L. and J. T. Overpeck. 2005. Is the Sonoran Desert losing its cool? Global Change Biology 11:2065-2077.

Williams, D. G. and Z. Baruch. 2000. African grass invasion in the Americas: ecosystem consequences and the role of ecophysiology. Biological Invasions 2:213-140.

Mexican Long-tongued Bat
(*Choeronycteris mexicana*)

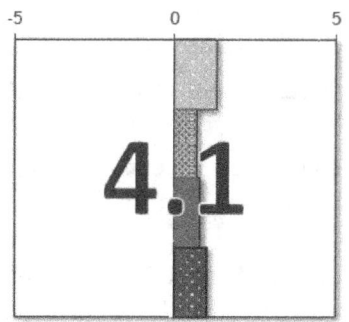

SUMMARY

Populations of Mexican long-tongued bats that occur in Arizona are females that migrate from Mexico to maternity colonies. Like the lesser long-nosed bat, this species is vulnerable to changes in temperature that will affect habitats and, in particular, flowering cacti and agave. Conversely, warmer winters will make conditions more favorable to year-round presence in the future. Fire, fuels, and invasive grass species management will be critical to this species.

VULNERABILITY	Score	Uncertainty
Habitat	**1.3**	14%
Physiology	**0.7**	67%
Phenology	**0.8**	0%
Interactions	**1.0**	20%
Overall	**4.1**	27%

Figure Key

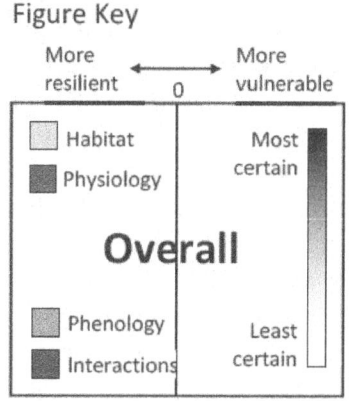

Introduction
Mexican long-tongued bat is a USFWS species of concern, a Forest Service sensitive species, and a species of greatest conservation need, Tier 1C, in Arizona State Wildlife Action Plan (AGFD 2006). Many aspects of this species' biology are not well known, but populations may be declining in Arizona (BISON-M). Individuals recorded in Arizona have been mostly females, but there are a few records of males in the United States (Balin 2009). Arizona populations are largely maternal roosting colonies, although it is rare to see more than 25 individuals together (Joaquin and others 1987). Similar in ecology to the lesser long-nosed bat, this species is nectivarous and migrates from U.S. locations to Mexico where it is generally a year-round resident. At the time of this report, there was no confirmation of this species on BMGR, but suitable habitat is present.

BMGR-East Climate and Projections
- Annual increase in temperature 2.2 °C (4 °F) by 2050 (www.climatewizard.org, A2 emissions, ensembled GCM) and greater evaporation
- No change in average rainfall by 2050 (www.climatewizard.org, A2 emissions, ensembled GCM)
- Sonoran Desert expands northward and eastward, and contracts in the southeast (Weiss and Overpeck 2005)
- More droughts and intense storms (Seager and others 2007)
- Earlier and more intense flooding (Garfin and Lenart 2007; Seager and others 2007)
- Summer monsoon changes unknown (Mitchell and others 2002)
- Grasses favored over shrubs (Esser 1992)
- Increases in invasive grasses and fires (Esser 1992; Williams and Baruch 2000)

- Warmer temperatures and decreased soil moisture in Mexico (Liverman and O'Brien 1991)
- CAM plants (succulents and cacti) will be resilient to increasing temperatures (Smith and others 1984)

A detailed review of projections is in the "Projections of Climate, Disturbance, and Biotic Communities" section of the main text.

Other Threats and Interactions with Climate

Many historic locations for this species remain occupied in Arizona (Cryan and Bogan 2003). Thus, although rare, populations in Arizona may be relatively stable. Mexican long-tongued bat, however, is threatened by a number of factors expected to be exacerbated by future climate change.

Like most bats, Mexican long-tongued bat is vulnerable to roost disturbance (NatureServe 2009). Roost protection is complicated by disturbance at roost sites. It is unknown if this species is sensitive to gating like lesser long-nosed bats. Climate change will potentially increase roost disturbance by illegal immigrants. Increased droughts predicted under future climate scenarios will result in failure of agricultural crops and put stress on growing human populations. Buffering of climate impacts varies with factors such as irrigation and government programs, both of which predict that drought impacts will be less severe in the United States as compared to Mexico (Vásquez-León and others 2003). In the absence of alterations to immigration policies, increased illegal traffic at the international border is expected.

The greatest threat to bat foraging areas at a landscape level is the likely expansion of invasive grasses and the concurrent increase in fire occurrence with subsequent reduction in agaves and cacti. Buffelgrass (*Pennisetum ciliare*), in addition to other invasive plants, is rapidly expanding and is becoming increasingly problematic in the Sonoran Desert (Burquez-Montijo and others 2002). It was, and continues to be, introduced in the Sonoran desert to enhance livestock grazing with almost the entire Sonoran Desert ecosystem prone to buffelgrass invasion (Arriaga and others 2004). Fires occur more frequently in the dry biomass created, and burning encourages more buffelgrass (Arriaga and others 2004). The invasion of African grasses and accompanying alteration of fire regimes will be exacerbated by climate change. Although currently limited in distribution at BMGR, African grasses will not likely be limited by climate changes in this region, and any increase in fire and other disturbances will favor grasses at the expense of species prone to fire mortality such as cacti and agaves.

Research Needs

Critical resource requirements are not well known in this species, making effective management difficult. We found little information on the specific requirements for roosting locations, which will be important to identifying critical roost resources. Important foraging plants are also not well known in this species, although Mexican long-tongued bats are assumed to select a broader range of plants than lesser long-nosed bats. More study is needed to understand flexible, migratory behaviors in this species. Depending on how this flexibility occurs in populations or individuals, changes in migration might be expected to occur regularly resulting in observed population fluctuations at isolated locations.

Management Implications

Buffelgrass has only been found along roadways in limited locations at BMGR but spread is almost inevitable along these corridors. Drought and very arid regions of BMGR will limit expansion to some extent. The potential for increasing impacts from invasive African grasses and increasing fires warrants consideration in management planning and implementation of preventative actions. It will also be a major factor affecting populations while on wintering grounds in Mexico. Management related to post-fire rehabilitation should also include actions that encourage agaves and cacti in suitable areas. Cactus flowering timing also depends on size, thus management that encourages diversity of size could be used to extend flowering period (Bustamante and Búrquez 2008).

Measures to protect bat species in general, such as closure of mines and caves, will benefit this species. Timing changes in bat arrival and presence at BMGR related to climate change should be anticipated, and time restrictions on activities that span specific dates should be altered accordingly. In addition, identification and monitoring of suitable caves or mines is warranted as conditions become more favorable for these bats.

Habitat: Mexican long-tongued bat (*Choeronycteris mexicana*)

Trait/Quality	Question	Background Info & Explanation of Score	Points
1. Area and distribution: *breeding*	Is the area or location of the associated vegetation type used for breeding activities by this species expected to change?	In the United States, Mexican long-tongued bat breeds along the border region with Mexico. In Arizona, this species inhabits primarily the oak-pine belt at elevations ranging from 4000 to 6000 ft as well as saguaro-palo-verde desertscrub (BISON-M). Additionally, it is often associated with Madrean evergreen woodlands and semi-desert grasslands with agave species in this region (Cryan and Bogan 2003). Increasing fires and invasive grasses will likely reduce pine-oak habitats along with upward elevational shifts.	1
2. Area and distribution: *non-breeding*	Is the area or location of the associated vegetation type used for non-breeding activities by this species expected to change?	Individuals that breed in the United States are mostly females and, after breeding, migrate to Mexico for the winter (Joaquín and others 1987; BISON-M). Central Mexico vegetation associations include desert scrub and mixed pine-oak forest (NatureServe, 2009). These vegetation types are expected to be exposed to increased fires and invasive grasses.	1
3. Habitat components: *breeding*	Are specific habitat components required for breeding expected to change within associated vegetation type?	Maternity roosts are required and are usually found in caves or abandoned mines (NatureServe 2009). Availability not expected to change.	0
4. Habitat components: *non-breeding*	Are other specific habitat components required for survival during non-breeding periods expected to change within associated vegetation type?	Day and night roosts are also required for non-breeding individuals (BISON-M). Roost locations include buildings, rock fissures, and caves (NatureServe 2009). Availability not expected to change.	0
5. Habitat quality	Within habitats occupied, are features of the habitat associated with better reproductive success or survival expected to change?	None known.	0
6. Ability to colonize new areas	What is the potential for this species to disperse?	Highly mobile, although males and females have different dispersal patterns.	-1
7. Migratory or transitional habitats	Does this species require additional habitats during migration that are separated from breeding and non-breeding habitats?	Populations in Arizona are migratory.	1

Physiology: Mexican long-tongued bat (*Choeronycteris mexicana*)

Trait/Quality	Question	Background Info & Explanation of Score	Points
1. Physiological thresholds	Are limiting physiological conditions expected to change?	Limited information. Range extends from southern California, Arizona, and southwest New Mexico southward into central Mexico and into Central America (Joaquín and others 1987). This species is limited in occupation of Arizona habitats because of cold limitations. Warmer temperatures may create more favorable conditions.	-1
2. Sex ratio	Is sex ratio determined by temperature?	No.	0
3. Exposure to weather-related disturbance	Are disturbance events (e.g., severe storms, fires, floods) that affect survival or reproduction expected to change?	Fire or other extreme weather is unlikely to result in direct mortality. Roosts are somewhat protected from disturbance, although there have been incidences of flooding of roosts and bat mortality in some species. Heavy rainfall events, which are expected to increase, are associated with mortality in some species and have been documented at Carlsbad Caverns, New Mexico. Flood risk at specific BMGR roosts is unknown.	1
4. Limitations to daily activity period	Are projected temperature or precipitation regimes that influence activity period of species expected to change?	Active at night. No information on limitations to foraging on hot nights. Rests part of the night in night roosts. Activity periods will probably not be reduced or increased.	0
5. Survival during resource fluctuation	Does this species have flexible strategies to cope with variation in resources across multiple years?	Seems to have somewhat flexible migration. Not known if this flexibility is possessed within individuals or within certain populations. All bats in Arizona are migratory, and it is not known if they would not migrate if flowering failed. Possible, but too little information to assume flexibility.	1
6. Metabolic rates	What is this species metabolic rate?	Moderate endothermic.	0

Phenology: Mexican long-tongued bat (*Choeronycteris mexicana*)

Trait/Quality	Question	Background Info & Explanation of Score	Points
1. Cues	Does this species use temperature or moisture cues to initiate activities related to fecundity or survival (e.g.,, hibernation, migration, breeding)?	Cues are likely a combination of internal and external signals. Does not hibernate.	0
2. Breeding timing	Are activities related to species' fecundity or survival tied to discrete resource peaks (e.g., food, breeding sites) that are expected to change?	Births in Arizona occur between mid June and early July (BISON-M) and may be timed to peak flowering. Earlier flowering has been documented in many Sonoran Desert plant species, including columnar cacti and agave (Bustamante and Búrquez 2008).	1

Phenology: Mexican long-tongued bat (*Choeronycteris mexicana*)

Trait/Quality	Question	Background Info & Explanation of Score	Points
3. Mismatch potential	What is the separation in time or space between cues that initiate activities related to survival or fecundity and discrete events that provide critical resources?	These bats follow the sequential flowering of agave, saguaro, ocotillo, palo verde, and prickly pear cactus (Fleming 1988). Migrations are described as following the sequential flowering of various cacti species (Fleming 1988).	-1
4. Resilience to timing mismatches during breeding	Is reproduction in this species more likely to co-occur with important events?	One reproductive event per year.	1

Biotic Interactions: Mexican long-tongued bat (*Choeronycteris mexicana*)

Trait/Quality	Question	Background Info & Explanation of Score	Points
1. Food resources	Are important food resources for this species expected to change?	Consume nectar and pollen from flowering plants, such as agaves and saguaro, and may supplement their diet with cactus fruit and insects (BISON-M). Mexican long-tongued bats may be able to feed on a greater variety of flowers than lesser long-nosed bats because of their longer tongues (BISON-M). In Arizona, large numbers of bats are thought to rely on hummingbird feeders before and after agave flowering season (BISON-M). Flowering and, thus, nectar availability generally decreases under dry conditions. In addition, more variable rainfall may increase variability in flowering.	1
2. Predators	Are important predator populations expected to change?	Limited information on predators, but known to be preyed upon by owls (Joaquín and others 1987). Predation rates not likely to change.	0
3. Symbionts	Are populations of symbiotic species expected to change?	No symbionts.	0
4. Disease	Is prevalence of diseases known to cause widespread mortality or reproductive failure in this species expected to change?	Rabies has been found in this species in Mexico and, while it can result in bat mortality, rabies is not common and generally not considered to be a significant threat to bat populations (Gillette and Kimbrough 1970). Another emerging bat disease is white-nose syndrome, which has been killing large numbers of roosting bats in northeastern North America. So far, it appears this disease only threatens hibernating species and is associated with cold conditions (Blehert and others 2008). Mexican long-tongued bats have neither of these risk factors.	0
5. Competitors	Are populations of important competing species expected to change?	Other nocturnal nectarivores that exploit these nectar resources are much smaller (e.g., moths and birds), so probably little competition. Could be competition with other bats, but lesser long-nosed bat probably exploits additional flower resources with its longer tongue. Expected to be similarly affected by climate change.	0

Literature Cited

Arizona Game and Fish Department. 2006. DRAFT. Arizona's Comprehensive Wildlife Conservation Strategy: 2005-2015. Arizona Game and Fish Department, Phoenix, AZ.

Arita, H. T. 1993. Conservation biology of the cave bats of Mexico. Journal of Mammalogy 74:693-702.

Arriaga, L., A. Castellanos, V. E. Moreno, and J. Alarcon. 2004. Potential ecological distribution of alien invasive species and risk assessment: a case study of buffel grass in arid regions of Mexico. Conservation Biology 18:1504-1514.

Bagne, K. E., M. M. Friggens, and D. M. Finch. 2011. A system for assessing vulnerability of species (SAVS) to climate change. USDA Forest Service, Rocky Mountain Research Station, Gen. Tech. Rep. RMRS-GTR-257.

Balin, 2009. Mexican long-tongued bat (*Choeronycteris mexicana*) in El Paso, Texas. Southwestern Naturalist 54:225-226.

BISON-M. Biotic Information System of New Mexico. New Mexico Game and Fish Department. Online at: http://www.bison-m.org.

Blehert, D. S., A. C. Hicks, M. Behr, C. U. Meteyer, B. M. Berlowski-Zier, and E. L. Buckles. 2008. Bat white-nose syndrome: an emerging fungal pathogen? SciencExpress. Published online October 30, 2008; 10.1123/science.11638.

Burquez-Montijo, A., M. Miller, and A. Martinez-Yrizar. 2002. Mexican grasslands, thornscrub, and the transformation of the Sonoran Desert by invasive exotic buffelgrass. Pages 126-146 In B. Tellman, ed., Arizona-Sonoran Desert Museum Studies in Natural History, Tucson, AZ.

Bustamante, E. and A. Búrquez. 2008. Effects of plant size and weather on the flowering phenology of the organ pipe cactus (*Stenocereus thurberi*). 102:1019-30.

Cryan, P. M. and M. A. Bogan. 2003. Recurrence of Mexican long-tongued bats (*Choeronycteris mexicana*) at historical sites in Arizona and New Mexico. Western North American Naturalist 63:314-319.

Environment and Natural Resources Division. December 2006. Programmic Biological Assessment for Ongoing and Future Military Operations and Activities at Fort Huachuca, Arizona.

Esser, G. 1992. Implications of climate change for production and decomposition in grasslands and coniferous forests. Ecological Applications 2:47-54.

Fleming, T. H. 1988. Evolution and ecology of phyllostomid bats. Pages 1-34 In The Short-Tailed Bat: A Study in Plant-Animal Interactions. The University of Chicago Press, Chicago.

Garfin, G. and M. Lenart. 2007. Climate change effects on Southwest water resources. Southwest Hydrology 6:16-17.

Gillette, D. D. and J. D. Kimbrough. 1970. Chiropteran Mortality. In B. Slaugher and D. Walton, eds., About Bats. Southern Methodist University Press, Dallas, TX.

Graham, E. A. and P. S. Nobel. 1996. Long term effects of a doubled atomospheric CO_2 concentration on the CAM species *Agave deserti*. Journal of Experimental Botany 47:61-69.

Joaquín, A-C, R. R. Hollander, and J. K. Jones, Jr. *Choeronycteris mexicana*. Mammalian Species 291:1-5.

Liverman, D. M. and K. L. O'Brien. 1991. Global warming and climate change in Mexico. Pages 351-364 In Global Environmental Change. Butterworth-Heinemann Ltd.

McLaughlin, S. E. and J. P. Bowers. 1982. Effects of wildfire on a Sonoran Desert plant community. Ecology 63:246-248.

Mitchell, D. L., D. Ivanova, R. Rabin, K. Redmond, and T. J. Brown. 2002. Gulf of California sea surface temperatures and the North American monsoon: mechanistic implications from observations. Journal of Climate 15:2261-2281.

NatureServe. 2009. NatureServe Explorer: an online encyclopedia of life [web application]. Version 7.1. NatureServe, Arlington, Virginia. Online at: http://www.natureserve.org/explorer. (Accessed: July 12, 2010)

Seager, R., T. Ming, I. Held, [and others]. 2007. Model projections of an imminent transition to a more arid climate in southwestern North America. Science 316:1181-1184.

Smith, S. D., B. Didden-Zopfy, and P. S. Nobel. 1984. High-temperature responses of North American cacti. Ecology 65:643-651.

Vásquez-León, M., C. T. West, and T. J. Finan. 2003. A comparative assessment of climate vulnerability: agriculture and ranching on both sides of the US-Mexico border. Global Environmental Change 13:159-173.

Weiss, J. L. and J. T. Overpeck. 2005. Is the Sonoran Desert losing its cool? Global Change Biology 11:2065-2077.

Williams, D. G. and Z. Baruch. 2000. African grass invasion in the Americas: ecosystem consequences and the role of ecophysiology. Biological Invasions 2:213-140.

Lesser Long-nosed Bat
(*Leptonycteris yerbabuenae*)

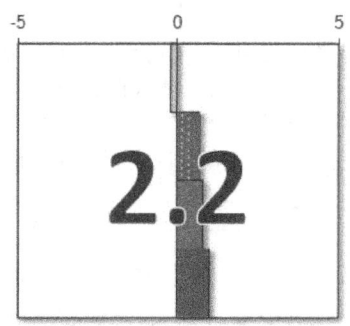

SUMMARY

Lesser long-nosed bat was assessed as moderately vulnerable to declines related to global climate change. Vulnerability is increased by reliance on quantity and timing of flowering of a limited number of plant species, while resilience is incurred by flexible migratory behaviors and probable resilience of forage plant populations to increasing temperatures. Unfortunately, changes in climate are expected to exacerbate current threats, making conservation of this species more challenging. Although few individuals of this species have been recorded at BMGR, current critical threats of roost disturbance and loss of foraging habitats will likely be increased through growing international border activity as well as the interactive effects of fire occurrence and non-native invasive grasses.

VULNERABILITY	Score	Uncertainty
Habitat	**-0.2**	14%
Physiology	**0.7**	33%
Phenology	**0.8**	0%
Interactions	**1.0**	0%
Overall	**2.2**	14%

Figure Key

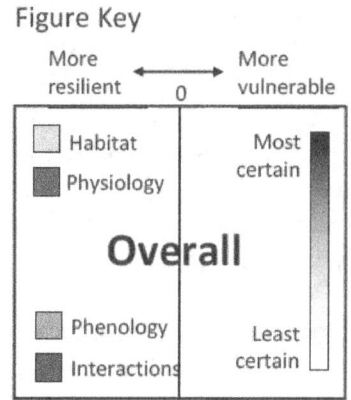

Introduction

Lesser long-nosed bat was listed in 1988 as endangered under the subspecies *Leptonycteris curasoae yerbabuenae*. Originally, they were listed as *Leptonycteris sanborni* (Sanborn's bat), but was also sometimes identified as *Leptonycteris curasoae*. Numbers of lesser long-nosed bats have increased in recent years or may not have been as low as reported when first listed. The five-year review by USFWS suggested downlisting the status to threatened because current populations appear to be stable or increasing, but the review also acknowledged that threats still exist, particularly for roosts, impacts in Mexico, and vulnerability of foraging plants to fire and invasive species (USFWS 2005). Populations are migratory from Mexico where there are also resident populations of this species (USFWS 2005). In this account, we focus on the migratory group that lives in Arizona and southern Sonora.

Only 3 maternity roosts and approximately 40 roosts overall are known in the United States (USFWS 2005). At BMGR, no roosting colonies have been found, and there have been few lesser long-nosed bats recorded, although the Sand Tank Mountains are thought to have good foraging and roosting habitats (Hall and others 2001). There are large maternity colonies in surrounding areas such as Cabeza Prieta National Wildlife Refuge, Organ Pipe Cactus National Monument, and the Tohono O'odham Reservation. BMGR may serve as foraging habitat for migrating individuals.

BMGR-East Climate and Projections

- Annual increase in temperature 2.2 °C (4 °F) by 2050 (www.climatewizard.org, A2 emissions, ensembled GCM) and greater evaporation
- No change in average rainfall by 2050 (www.climatewizard.org, A2 emissions, ensembled GCM)
- Sonoran Desert expands northward and eastward, and contracts in the southeast (Weiss and Overpeck 2005)
- More droughts and intense storms (Seager and others 2007)
- Earlier and more intense flooding (Garfin and Lenart 2007; Seager and others 2007)
- Summer monsoon changes unknown (Mitchell and others 2002)
- Grasses favored over shrubs (Esser 1992)
- Increases in invasive grasses and fires (Esser 1992; Williams and Baruch 2000)
- Warmer temperatures and decreased soil moisture in Mexico (Liverman and O'Brien 1991)
- CAM plants (succulents and cacti) will be resilient to increasing temperatures (Smith and others 1984)

A detailed review of projections is in the "Projections of Climate, Disturbance, and Biotic Communities" section of the main text.

Other Threats and Interactions with Climate

There are many known threats to this species. Suitable concentrations of food plants and day roosts are considered critical (Fleming 1995). The USFWS five-year review identified illegal border activity, fire, and drought as important threats to roosts or foraging habitats (USFWS 2005). The review further noted that grazing, tequila harvesting, and prescribed fire are probably not substantial threats in the United States. (USFWS 2005). Urban development, wind farms, and changing fire regimes are additional potential threats that have yet to be addressed as part of recovery planning. Climate change impacts were not specifically addressed in the review.

Roost protection is complicated by disturbance at roost sites. There are also issues with gating cave and mine entrances, including gate vandalism and bat avoidance after gating (USFWS 2005). Lesser long-nosed bats may be sensitive to gate construction and configuration. Climate change will also potentially increase roost disturbance by illegal immigrants. Increased droughts predicted under future climate scenarios will result in failure of agricultural crops and stress growing human populations. Buffering of climate impacts varies with factors such as irrigation and government programs, both of which predict that drought impacts will be less severe in the United States as compared to Mexico (Vásquez-León and others 2003). In the absence of alterations to immigration policies, increased illegal traffic at the international border is expected.

Climate change may create timing mismatches between species and resources. A number of observations and studies have found there is not close synchrony between lesser long-nosed bat arrival in Arizona and New Mexico with the peak of agave flowering (Fleming and others 2001; Scott 2004). Bat arrival late in agave blooming may allow flexibility in earlier bat arrival, although advancement of blooming may be problematic if bat migration cannot advance equally (see Table A1). Observations of timing, however, are limited and generally occurred only over short time periods, so it is reasonable to assume there is annual variability of arrival, flowering, and, therefore, the synchrony of these events.

Timing and the extent of synchronicity in flowering of forage species along migratory routes will affect population sizes and arrival dates in Arizona, at least as observed from a single location such as BMGR. Migratory and non-migratory demes probably make the species more resilient as a whole to climate and resource variability. More critical to populations is failure of flowering, particularly if synchronous across their range. In one study, monsoons were found to be generally asynchronous between northern Mexico and the

Table A1. Event timing and lesser long-nosed bat (LLNB) populations in northern Mexico (MX), southern Arizona (AZ), and New Mexico (NM). Dates of recorded events are listed by month with sources, including recording year and location of observation, noted below.

	JAN	FEB	MAR	APR	MAY	JUN	JUL	AUG	SEP	OCT	NOV	DEC
Saguaro blooming MX			?[a]	1-30[a]	late[a]							
Agave blooming MX			1-31[b]	1-30[b]	1-31[b]	1-30[b]	1-31[b]	1-mid[b]				
LLNB presence MX			?[a] ?[c]	1-30[a] 1-30[c]	1-mid?[a] 1-end[c]							
Saguaro blooming AZ/NM				late[d]	1-31[d]	early[d]						
Agave blooming AZ/NM						18-30[e] late[f]	1-31[e] 1-31[f]	1-31[e] 1-31[f]	1-12[e] 1-30[f]	early[f]		
LLNB arrival AZ/NM							14-?[i]	24-31[e] ~9[g] 2-7[h]	1-12[e]			

Sources:
[a] Fleming 2001 (1995-1996, Bahia de Kino, Sonora, MX)
[b] Fleming 1993 (?, numerous locations, MX)
[c] Horner and others 1998 (1989-1990, Bahia de Kino, Sonora, MX)
[d] Fleming 2001 (1997, Organ Pipe, AZ)
[e] Scott 2004 (1997, Chiricahuas, AZ)
[f] Slauson 2000 (1993-1994, southern AZ)
[g] Cockrum 1991 (13 year average, Chiricahua Mountains, AZ)
[h] Ober and Steidl 2004 (1999 Huachuca Mountains, AZ)
[i] Beatty 1955 (?, AZ)

southwestern United States (Comrie and Glenn 1998), thus adequate resources should be available within some part of the range. Monsoon behavior under current climate projections, however, is unpredictable at this point and past patterns may not extend into the future. Interestingly, there is some evidence that seed set of agaves was higher in the past (Howell and Roth 1981), a factor that is likely affected by climate. It is also possible that there was greater synchronicity between bat arrival and flowering in the past.

BMGR has saguaro (*Cereus giganteus*) and other large cactus species as well as desert agave (*Agave deserti*). Lesser long-nosed bats use clumped concentrations of agaves rather than isolated individuals (Ober and Steidl 2004). The greatest threat to bat foraging areas at a landscape level is the likely expansion of invasive grasses and the concurrent increase in fire occurrence with subsequent reduction in agaves and cacti. Buffelgrass (*Pennisetum ciliare*), in addition to the already common red brome (*Bromus rubens*), is rapidly expanding and is becoming increasingly problematic in the Sonoran Desert. It was, and continues to be, introduced in the Sonoran Desert to enhance livestock grazing although almost the entire Sonoran Desert ecosystem is prone to buffelgrass invasion (Arriaga and others 2004). The invasion of African grasses and accompanying alteration of fire regimes will be exacerbated by climate change. African grasses will likely not be limited by climate changes in this region, and any increase in fire and other disturbances will favor further conversion to grasslands.

Part of the U.S. strategy to combat increasing CO_2 levels is to promote alternative energy sources. Wind farms are increasingly being proposed in many areas, including the Southwest. Wind turbines are known to kill bats (Arnett and others 2008), but to date, there has been no documented mortality for lesser long-nosed bat. Potential for impacts will be, at least in part, related to wind farm locations and their proximity to bat roosts, migratory routes, or foraging areas.

Research Needs
Several areas of deficient information on lesser long-nosed bat were identified in the USFWS five-year review, including: bat response to gates and other methods aimed at preventing roost disturbance, wind farm impacts, overall population size, and long-term effects of fire on foraging resources (USFWS 2005).

Additional research needs identified by this assessment follow. Of particular interest is how fluctuations in flowering timing alter bat migratory behavior and timing of arrival throughout the U.S. range and, in particular, BMGR. In addition, little is known about how climate variability may affect flowering variability, particularly across latitudes where the bat occurs, and if variables related to flowering influence bat survival. Information on the interactions among warming climate, fire, and expansion of invasive grasses will be valuable in identifying effective management actions. Information is also needed on bat mortality and wind turbines, as well as on management options that reduce populations of African grasses and probability of spread.

Management Implications
Lesser long-nosed bat only spends a portion of the year on BMGR. Activities in Mexico, where this species winters, will affect populations that migrate to Arizona.

Presence of the lesser long-nosed bat at BMGR is tied to the birth of young at nearby maternity caves and the blooming of columnar cactus and agave. The potential for increasing impacts from invasive African grasses and increasing fires on cacti and agaves warrants consideration in management planning and implementation of preventative actions. Management related to post-fire rehabilitation should also plan for and implement actions that encourage cacti and agaves while discouraging further spread of invasive plants. Encouragement of diverse cactus size may also help to extend the flowering season (Bustamante and Búrquez 2008).

Anticipated changes in bat arrival and use of BMGR with climate change indicates the need to reevaluate any time restrictions on activities that span specific dates meant to protect bats. Gates at roosts also should be evaluated as this species is sensitive to their configuration. Any potential roosts on BMGR should be identified and monitored.

Habitat: Lesser long-nosed bat (*Leptonycteris yerbabuenae*)			
Trait/Quality	**Question**	**Background Info & Explanation of Score**	**Points**
1. Area and distribution: *breeding*	Is the area or location of the associated vegetation type used for breeding activities by this species expected to change?	Lesser long-nosed bats primarily occupy Sonoran Desert vegetation along with a variety of woodlands, grasslands, and shrublands where food resources are available. Climate projections indicate possible expansion of the Sonoran Desert northward as temperatures warm (Weiss and Overpeck 2005). Accordingly, expansion of available habitat for lesser long-nosed bat might be inferred, but other important issues are to be considered. Expansion will be limited by projected increases in fire frequency and increases in invasive grass species that will both be favored by a warming climate. No overall change in area projected.	0
2. Area and distribution: *non-breeding*	Is the area or location of the associated vegetation type used for non-breeding activities by this species expected to change?	Non-breeding areas will likely be reduced with decreases in Sonoran Desert habitats to the south in Mexico predicted by temperature and precipitation projections in addition to the interacting effects of invasive grasses and fire occurrence. Sonoran Desert is projected to decline in the southern portions of the range (Weiss and Overpeck 2005). Active conversion of Sonoran Desert to grasslands and projected increases in fires make further loss of habitat area likely.	1
3. Habitat components: *breeding*	Are specific habitat components required for breeding expected to change within associated vegetation type?	Several types of roosts are used: day roosts, maternity roosts, bachelor roosts, and temporary night roosts. Roosts are often in caves or abandoned mines. Maternity roosts are not known to occur on BMGR. Roosts are of variable types and microclimates. Climate unlikely to affect availability of suitable roosts.	0
4. Habitat components: *non-breeding*	Are other specific habitat components required for survival during non-breeding periods expected to change within associated vegetation type?	Roosts are often in caves or abandoned mines. Individuals require multiple roost types at different locations. Thought to use roosts with a variety of microclimates, so it is unlikely that warmer temperatures will decrease roost availability.	0
5. Habitat quality	Within habitats occupied, are features of the habitat associated with better reproductive success or survival expected to change?	Warmer maternity caves associated with better development of young (Arends and others 1995). May benefit from rising temperatures.	-1
6. Ability to colonize new areas	What is the potential for this species to disperse?	Migratory and highly mobile moving over large areas to feed.	-1
7. Migratory or transitional habitats	Does this species require additional habitats during migration that are separated from breeding and non-breeding habitats?	For Arizona, this species is a long-distance migrant. Some populations remain resident in Mexico. Migratory behavior is thought to take advantage of periodic resources (USFWS 1995). Males and females follow progressive flowering of columnar cacti and paniculate agaves. Although highly mobile, they avoid crossing high-density urban housing (USFWS 2005).	1

Physiology: Lesser long-nosed bat (*Leptonycteris yerbabuenae*)			
Trait/Quality	Question	Background Info & Explanation of Score	Points
1. Physiological thresholds	Are limiting physiological conditions expected to change?	Lesser long-nosed bats have a lower critical temperature of 30.5 °C and generally seek warm conditions (Fleming and others 1998). They often roost colonially in caves that trap metabolic heat, but have been found in a variety of different roost conditions (USFWS 1995). Migratory females give birth in Arizona, and warmer maternity roosts may increase growth rates of the young (Arends and others 1995). Leave United States because of cold winter conditions and seem well suited to desert conditions with a fairly high lower critical temperature. While projected changes are not expected to exceed physiological thresholds, they may instead reduce cold periods, which are unsuitable.	-1
2. Sex ratio	Is sex ratio determined by temperature?	No.	0
3. Exposure to weather-related disturbance	Are disturbance events (e.g., severe storms, fires, floods) that affect survival or reproduction expected to change?	Heavy rainfall events, which are expected to increase, are associated with mortality in some species—documented at Carlsbad Caverns. Although BMGR has no known roosts, individuals that forage on BMGR may use roosts that are prone to flooding (risk unknown).	1
4. Limitations to daily activity period	Are projected temperature or precipitation regimes that influence activity period of species expected to change?	Species can fly long distances between roosts and foraging sites (from 50-100 km; USFWS 1995). Although distance from roosts to foraging areas is considered an important component of energy expenditure, lesser long-nosed bats have also been found to be efficient fliers and well adapted to performing long, daily commutes (Horner and others 1998). Active at night. Rest part of the night in night roosts, but no information on limitations to foraging on hot nights. Although distance between roost sites and foraging locations may be affected, there is no anticipated effect because apparently do not need to expend large amounts of energy to forage at distant locations.	0
5. Survival during resource fluctuation	Does this species have flexible strategies to cope with variation in resources across multiple years?	Migratory behavior seems to be variable with both migratory and sedentary strategies that may be an adaptation to highly variable flowering resources (Rojas-Martinez and others 1999). Occurrence of migratory and non-migratory demes related to resource availability and likely helpful with fluctuating resources. All individuals at BMGR, however, are migratory, so these populations do not possess this alternative, and plasticity in behavior within demes is unknown.	1
6. Metabolic rates	What is this species metabolic rate?	Moderate endothermic.	0

Phenology: Lesser long-nosed bat (*Leptonycteris yerbabuenae*)			
Trait/Quality	Question	Background Info & Explanation of Score	Points
1. Cues	Does this species use temperature or moisture cues to initiate activities related to fecundity or survival (e.g., hibernation, migration, breeding)?	Do not hibernate. Probably initiate migration based on flowering resources, but it may also be related to progress of pregnancy in females. No direct moisture or temperature cues known.	0
2. Breeding timing	Are activities related to species' fecundity or survival tied to discrete resource peaks (e.g., food, breeding sites) that are expected to change?	Migratory females arrive in Arizona pregnant and give birth to one young that can fly at about 4 weeks. Birth is not highly synchronous among individuals at the same maternity cave, as pregnant females co-occur with females with young that are ready to fly (USFWS 1995). Females that do not migrate give birth in winter in Mexico (USFWS 2005). Migration and breeding is tied to flowering timing, which is likely to be altered by changes in temperature and precipitation.	1
3. Mismatch potential	What is the separation in time or space between cues that initiate activities related to survival or fecundity and discrete events that provide critical resources?	Lesser long-nosed bats are present April to November in Arizona, although this seems to vary by year. Movements coincide with blooming (cactus in the spring and agave in the summer). Likely that this species' movements are directly related to presence of nectar resources, thus has the potential to respond quickly to changes.	-1
4. Resilience to timing mismatches during breeding	Is reproduction in this species more likely to co-occur with important events?	One reproductive event per year.	1

Biotic Interactions: Lesser long-nosed bat (*Leptonycteris yerbabuenae*)			
Trait/Quality	Question	Background Info & Explanation of Score	Points
1. Food resources	Are important food resources for this species expected to change?	Lesser long-nosed bats are adapted to feed on nectar and pollen of various columnar cactus and paniculate agave species. They are able to switch between various cactus and agave species when flowering of one species fails. Also may eat insects and fruits and have been observed to use hummingbird feeders (USFWS 2005). Northern migrants eat almost exclusively CAM plants (agaves and cacti). Because of their ability to open their stomates at night, CAM plants are well adapted to dry conditions. In Mexico, lesser long-nosed bats are known to feed on C_3 plants (most shrubs and forbs) as well (Fleming and others 1993). Species on BMGR are primarily saguaro and desert agave. These CAM plants are resilient to dry conditions, but flowering and thus nectar availability generally decreases under dry conditions. In addition, more variable rainfall may increase variability in flowering.	1

Biotic Interactions: Lesser long-nosed bat (*Leptonycteris yerbabuenae*)			
Trait/Quality	**Question**	**Background Info & Explanation of Score**	**Points**
2. Predators	Are important predator populations expected to change?	Few incidences of predation have been documented and predators were various. No avoidance of activity during full moons suggests predation pressure while foraging is not strong (USFWS 1995). There is a potential for large impacts of single predators at small roosts, but overall predation probably has little impact on populations.	0
3. Symbionts	Are populations of symbiotic species expected to change?	This species is an important, but not exclusive, pollinator and seed disperser for these plants. Some researchers cite close association and bat adaptations in paniculate agaves and columnar cacti as evidence for a tight mutualistic relationship, but others have noted that this relationship is likely not as strong in the southwestern United States and northwest Mexico as in areas where nectar-feeding bats occur year-round (Fleming and others 2001). Foraging plant populations expected to survive warmer temperatures and reduced rainfall.	0
4. Disease	Is prevalence of diseases known to cause widespread mortality or reproductive failure in this species expected to change?	Rabies has been found in this species in Mexico and, while it can result in bat mortality, rabies is not common and generally not considered to be a significant threat to bat populations (Gillette and Kimbrough 1970). Another emerging bat disease is white-nose syndrome, which has been killing large numbers of roosting bats in northeastern North America. So far, it appears this disease only threatens hibernating species and is associated with cold conditions (Blehert and others 2008). Lesser long-nosed bats have neither of these risk factors.	0
5. Competitors	Are populations of important competing species expected to change?	Lesser long-nosed bats roost with a variety of other bats in Mexico (Arita 1993) and do not appear to segregate from other bat species at roosts. Other nocturnal nectarivores that exploit these nectar resources are much smaller (e.g., moths and birds), so probably little competition. Could compete with other nectarivorous bats, but Mexican long-tongued bat probably exploits additional flower resources with its longer tongue. Expected to be similarly affected by climate change.	0

Literature Cited

Arita, H. T. 1993. Conservation biology of the cave bats of Mexico. Journal of Mammalogy 74:693-702.

Arends, A., F. J. Bonaccorso, and M. Genoud. 1995. Basal rates of metabolism of nectarivorous bats (Phyllostomidae) from a semiarid thorn forest in Venezuela. Journal of Mammalogy 76:947-956.

Arnett, E. B., W. Brown, W. P. Erickson, [and others]. 2008. Patterns of bat fatalities at wind energy facilities in North America. Journal of Wildlife Management 72:61-78.

Arriaga, L., A. Castellanos V., E. Moreno, and J. Alarcon. 2004. Potential ecological distribution of alien invasive species and risk assessment: a case study of buffel grass in arid regions of Mexico. Conservation Biology 18:1504-1514.

Bagne, K. E., M. M. Friggens, and D. M. Finch. 2011. A system for assessing vulnerability of species (SAVS) to climate change. USDA Forest Service, Rocky Mountain Research Station, Gen. Tech. Rep. RMRS-GTR-257.

Beatty, L. D. 1955. Autecology of the longnose bat, *Leptonycteris nivalis* (Saussure). Unpublished thesis, University of Arizona, Tucson. (Primary document unavailable; as referenced in Scott 2004.)

Blehert, D. S., A. C. Hicks, M. Behr, C. U. Meteyer, B. M. Berlowski-Zier, and E. L. Buckles. 2008. Bat white-nose syndrome: an emerging fungal pathogen? Sciencexpress. Published online October 30, 2008; 10.1123/science.11638.

Burquez-Montijo, A., M. Miller, and A. Martinez-Yrizar. 2002. Mexican grasslands, thornscrub, and the transformation of the Sonoran Desert by invasive exotic buffelgrass. Pages 126-146 In B. Tellman, ed., Arizona-Sonoran Desert Museum Studies in Natural History, Tucson, AZ.

Cockrum, E. L. 1991. Seasonal distribution of northwestern populations of the long-nosed bats, *Leptonycteris sanborni* Family Phyllostomidae. Anales del Instituto Biologica, Universidad Nacional Autonoma de Mexico, Serie Zoologica 62:181-202.

Comrie, A. C. and E. C. Glenn. 1998. Principal components-based regionalization of precipitation regimes across southwest United States and northern Mexico, with an application to monsoon precipitation variability. Climate Research 10:201-215.

Esser, G. 1992. Implications of climate change for production and decomposition in grasslands and coniferous forests. Ecological Applications 2:47-54.

Fleming, T. H., R. A. Nufiez, and L. L. Sternberg. 1993. Seasonal changes in the diets of migrant and non-migrant nectarivorous bats as revealed by carbon stable isotope analysis. Oecologia 94:72-75.

Fleming, T. H., A. A. Nelson, and V. M. Dalton. 1998. Roosting behavior of the lesser long-nosed bat, Leptonycteris curacoae. Journal of Mammalogy 79:147-155.

Fleming, T. H., C. T. Sahley, N. Holland, J. D. Nason, and J. L. Hamrick. 2001. Sonoran columnar cacti and the evolution of generalized pollination systems. Ecological Monographs 71:511-530.

Garfin, G. and M. Lenart. 2007. Climate change effects on Southwest water resources. Southwest Hydrology 6:16-17.

Gillette, D. D. and J. D. Kimbrough. 1970. Chiropteran Mortality. In B. Slaugher and D. Walton, eds., About Bats. Southern Methodist University Press, Dallas, TX.

Graham, E. A. and P. S. Nobel. 1996. Long term effects of a doubled atomospheric CO_2 concentration on the CAM species *Agave deserti*. Journal of Experimental Botany 47:61-69.

Horner M. A., T. H. Fleming, and C. T. Sahley. 1998. Foraging behaviour and energetics of a nectar-feeding bat, *Leptonycteris curasoae* (Chiroptera: Phyllostomidae). Journal of Zoology, London 244:575-586.

Howell, D. J. and B. S. Roth. 1981. Sexual reproduction in agaves: the benefits of bats; the cost of semelparous advertising. Ecology 62:1-7.

Liverman, D. M. and K. L. O'Brien. 1991. Global warming and climate change in Mexico. Pages 351-364 In Global Environmental Change. Butterworth-Heinemann Ltd.

Maurer, E. P., L. Brekke, T. Pruitt, and P. B. Duffy. 2007. Fine-resolution climate projections enhance regional climate change impact studies, Eos Trans. AGU, 88(47):504.

McLaughlin, S. E. and J. P. Bowers. 1982. Effects of wildfire on a Sonoran Desert plant community. Ecology 63:246-248.

Mitchell, D. L., D. Ivanova, R. Rabin, K. Redmond, and T. J. Brown. 2002. Gulf of California sea surface temperatures and the North American monsoon: mechanistic implications from observations. Journal of Climate 15:2261-2281.

Ober, H. K. and R. J. Steidl. 2004. Foraging rates of *Leptonycteris curasoae* vary with characteristics of *Agave palmeri*. Southwestern Naturalist 49:68-74.

Ober, H. K., R. J. Steidl, and V.M. Dalton. 2000. Foraging ecology of lesser long-nosed bats. Final Report to University of Arizona, School of Renewable Natural Resources, Tucson, AZ. 25 p.

Rojas-Martinez, A., A. Valiente-Banuet, M. del Coro Arizmendi, A. Alcantara-Eguren, and H. T. Arita. 1999. Seasonal distribution of the long-nosed bat (*Leptonycteris curasoae*) in North America: does a generalized migration pattern really exist? Journal of Biogeography 26:1065-1077.

Scott, P. 2004. Timing of *Agave palmeri* flowering and nectar-feeding bat visitation in the Peloncillos and Chiracahua Mountains. Southwestern Naturalist 49:425-434.

Seager, R., T. Ming, I. Held, [and others]. 2007. Model projections of an imminent transition to a more arid climate in southwestern North America. Science 316:1181-1184.

Slauson, L. A. 2000. Pollination biology of two chiropterophilous agaves in Arizona. American Journal of Botany 87:825-836.

U.S. Fish and Wildlife Service (USFWS). 1995. Recovery plan for the lesser long-nosed bat, *Leptonycteris curasoae yerbabuenae*. U.S. Fish and Wildlife Service, Albuquerque, NM. 45 p.

U.S. Fish and Wildlife Service (USFWS). 2005. Lesser long-nosed bat five year review: summary and evaluation. Prepared by Richardson, Scott. Arizona Ecological Service Office, Tucson, AZ.

Vásquez-León, M., C. T. West, and T. J. Finan. 2003. A comparative assessment of climate vulnerability: agriculture and ranching on both sides of the US-Mexico border. Global Environmental Change 13:159-173.

Van Devender, T. R. and M. A. Dimmitt. 2006. Final report on conservation of Arizona upland Sonoran Desert habitat: status and threats of buffelgrass (*Pennisetum ciliare*) in Arizona and Sonora. Arizona-Sonora Desert Museum, Tucson, AZ.

Weiss, J. L. and J. T. Overpeck. 2005. Is the Sonoran Desert losing its cool? Global Change Biology 11:2065-2077.

Williams, D. G. and Z. Baruch. 2000. African grass invasion in the Americas: ecosystem consequences and the role of ecophysiology. Biological Invasions 2:213-140.

Desert Bighorn Sheep
(*Ovis canadensis mexicana*)

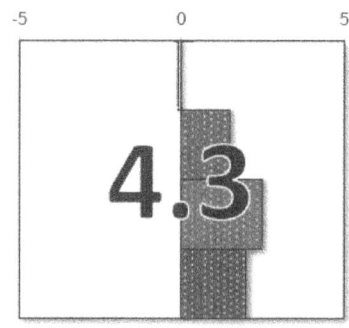

SUMMARY

Desert bighorn sheep has a number of characteristics that should aid survival during dry periods, which are expected to increase in the region with projected climate change. Overall, this species is predicted to be moderately vulnerable to detrimental effects of climate change. Water availability has important relationships with bighorn breeding and survival and is likely to be an increasingly critical issue. Management actions that can mitigate drought conditions should be considered, but the ability of artificial waters to buffer populations has not been demonstrated so far. Although not currently major threats in the Southwest, interactions of climate with predation and disease need investigation.

VULNERABILITY	Score	Uncertainty
Habitat	**-0.1**	29%
Physiology	**1.5**	33%
Phenology	**2.5**	25%
Interactions	**1.0**	40%
Overall	**4.3**	**32%**

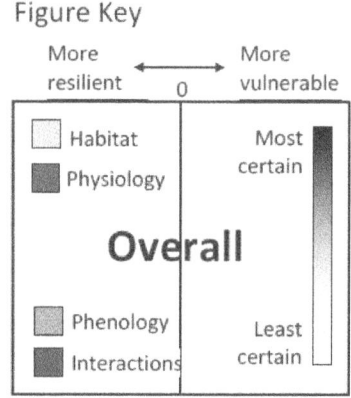

Figure Key

Introduction
There are four desert subspecies of bighorn sheep. The mexicana subspecies has no USFWS status but is designated as sensitive by the U.S. Forest Service and managed as a game species on BMGR. As of April 2009, hunting was closed on BMGR east of Highway 85 because of declining populations but remains open to the west of Highway 85.

BMGR-East Climate and Projections
- Annual increase in temperature 2.2 °C (4 °F) by 2050 (www.climatewizard.org, A2 emissions, ensembled GCM) and greater evaporation
- No change in average rainfall by 2050 (www.climatewizard.org, A2 emissions, ensembled GCM)
- Sonoran Desert expands northward and eastward, and contracts in the southeast (Weiss and Overpeck 2005)
- More droughts and intense storms (Seager and others 2007)
- Earlier and more intense flooding (Garfin and Lenart 2007; Seager and others 2007)
- Summer monsoon changes unknown (Mitchell and others 2002)
- Grasses favored over shrubs (Esser 1992)
- Increases in invasive grasses and fires (Esser 1992; Williams and Baruch 2000)
- Warmer temperatures and decreased soil moisture in Mexico (Liverman and O'Brien 1991)
- CAM plants (succulents and cacti) will be resilient to increasing temperatures (Smith and others 1984)

USDA Forest Service RMRS-GTR-284. 2012.

A detailed review of projections is in the "Projections of Climate, Disturbance, and Biotic Communities" section of the main text.

Other Threats and Interactions with Climate

Low population size in the desert bighorn sheep elevates even small mortality factors to critical stressors. Declines during drought periods may be regular occurrences (McKinney and others 2001), but low population size makes subsequent recovery slow and local extinctions more likely.

At Cabeza Prieta National Wildlife Refuge, presence of permanent water did not appear to affect bighorn sheep populations (Broyles and Cutler 1999). Water has been suggested as limiting to populations, particularly during hot periods, but water sources may also be a source of toxins or disease, attract predators, and increase human disturbance (see Broyles and Cutler 1999 for discussion). Conversely, bighorn sheep is documented to use artificial water sources, and mortality from dehydration might be inferred from several cases where dead individuals have been found at water sources that have gone dry. Water limitations may interact with issues of reduced forage during drought periods.

An analysis of California bighorn sheep metapopulations and predicted response to climate change found that elevation, permanent springs, and precipitation were important to persistence (Epps and others 2004). Metapopulations in drier, low-elevation areas were more vulnerable, which likely indicates that Arizona populations are vulnerable to a warming climate based on these same factors.

Research Needs

Predation and disease have been identified as important threats to desert bighorn, but interactions of these factors with climate are not well known. These interactions will be critical to anticipating climate change response. Ability of artificial waters to buffer populations from declines has not been demonstrated, but has also received only limited study.

Management Implications

A recent study by Cain and others (2008) did not find detrimental effects on survival or reproduction with removal of artificial water sources, but precipitation variation during the study made conclusions difficult. Artificial waters, however, did not prevent mortalities during drought conditions of the pre-treatment period. The question of managing wildlife by creating artificial water sources is becoming a more critical one. The current benefits of artificial waters to bighorn populations have not been well documented (Broyles 1995), but as temperatures increase, the potential benefit of artificial waters is increased as physiological thresholds are approached.

BMGR is closed to cattle grazing, which has minimized issues related to grazing competition and disease transmission. Some trespass grazing and grazing by feral burros occurs (BMGR 2003), but is unlikely to have significant or altered impacts with climate change unless there is increased contact with livestock that results in disease transmission, such as through attraction to a localized water source.

Habitat: Desert bighorn sheep (*Ovis canadensis mexicana*)

Trait/Quality	Question	Background Info & Explanation of Score	Points
1. Area and distribution: *breeding*	Is the area or location of the associated vegetation type used for breeding activities by this species expected to change?	Desert bighorn sheep are associated with a wide variety of vegetation types in rugged mountainous terrain, including juniper and desert scrub communities. In the Harqualaha Mountains, bighorn sheep were found to avoid permanent water and bajadas, while favoring areas with preferred browse species and open vegetation (Krausman and Leopold 1986). In addition, they have been associated with vegetation that included ocotillo (Krausman and others 1989). Relative proportions of grass, shrubs, and forbs expected to vary with increased temperatures plus interactions with fire and invasive plants, but suitable rugged mountain habitats expected to remain relatively unchanged.	0
2. Area and distribution: *non-breeding*	Is the area or location of the associated vegetation type used for non-breeding activities by this species expected to change?	Same as above.	0
3. Habitat components: *breeding*	Are specific habitat components required for breeding expected to change within associated vegetation type?	None known.	0
4. Habitat components: *non-breeding*	Are other specific habitat components required for survival during non-breeding periods expected to change within associated vegetation type?	Barrel cacti may be an important water source during hot periods (Warrick and Krausman 1989). It has been suggested that these benefits may be lost during dry periods when cacti become dehydrated. Cacti can lose up to 81% of their water after being dehydrated for 18 months and still survive (Barcikowski and Nobel 1984), but presumably, the benefits from eating dessicated cactus would be reduced.	0
5. Habitat quality	Within habitats occupied, are features of the habitat associated with better reproductive success or survival expected to change?	For *Ovis canadensis nelsoni* in Nevada, higher precipitation in September to December had a positive effect on lamb survival the following year, presumably through increased plant growth (Douglas and Leslie 1986). Higher winter precipitation was also associated with population increases in Arizona (McKinney and others 2001). Lower lamb survival has been associated with lower quality of forage (Krausman and others 1988). Winter precipitation expected to be unchanged, but soil moisture available to plants reduced with warmer temperatures. Many vegetation characteristics may relate to predator avoidance, which may be increased in open vegetation types where visibility is improved. Other studies have also found a positive association of bighorn sheep presence and escape terrain (Andrew and others 1999; McKinney and others 2003). There is little quantitative data, however, on the relation between survival and landscape variables presumably associated with predator avoidance. More open vegetation types and abiotic features may increase predator detection and increase survival. Cacti or other succulent plants may be important for surviving dry periods. Cacti are relatively	1

Habitat: Desert bighorn sheep (*Ovis canadensis mexicana*)

Trait/Quality	Question	Background Info & Explanation of Score	Points
		resistant to drought conditions. Most associations expected to remain unchanged, but quality of forage is expected to be more variable as rainfall becomes more variable.	
6. Ability to colonize new areas	What is the potential for this species to disperse?	Highly mobile.	-1
7. Migratory or transitional habitats	Does this species require additional habitats during migration that are separated from breeding and non-breeding habitats?	Seasonal movements, but no additional habitats required.	0

Physiology: Desert bighorn sheep (*Ovis canadensis mexicana*)

Trait/Quality	Question	Background Info & Explanation of Score	Points
1. Physiological thresholds	Are limiting physiological conditions expected to change?	Desert bighorn sheep are well adapted to water limitations and have the ability to reduce water losses from urine and feces, absorb water into the bloodstream rapidly, and have red blood cells resistant to osmotic stress (Hansen 1982). There is disagreement over the importance of water for the subspecies (Smith and Krausman 1988; Broyles and Cutler 1999). Drought years are associated with reduced populations and lower survival rates (McKinney and others 2001). Observed mortality during droughts historically indicates that this species may not tolerate further temperature increases or moisture stress.	1
2. Sex ratio	Is sex ratio determined by temperature?	No.	0
3. Exposure to weather-related disturbance	Are disturbance events (e.g., severe storms, fires, floods) that affect survival or reproduction expected to change?	No known mortality from disturbance events, although some likely occurs.	0
4. Limitations to daily activity period	Are projected temperature or precipitation regimes that influence activity period of species expected to change?	Actively seek shade and may spend more time inactive when temperatures are high. Higher temperatures may reduce activities or movements.	1
5. Survival during resource fluctuation	Does this species have flexible strategies to cope with variation in resources across multiple years?	Some studies have found breeding can extend to most of the year, but that the majority of lambs are born in the spring (Rubin and others 2000). An extended reproductive period may be advantageous to variable conditions. This may be advantageous for increasing variability in rainfall.	-1
6. Metabolic rates	What is this species metabolic rate?	Moderate.	0

Phenology: Desert bighorn sheep (*Ovis canadensis mexicana*)

Trait/Quality	Question	Background Info & Explanation of Score	Points
1. Cues	Does this species use temperature or moisture cues to initiate activities related to fecundity or survival (e.g., hibernation, migration, breeding)?	Not known what triggers breeding, but at least partly internal.	0
2. Breeding timing	Are activities related to species' fecundity or survival tied to discrete resource peaks (e.g., food, breeding sites) that are expected to change?	In the Harqualaha Mountains, lambs were born from January to June (Krausman 1989). In California, most young were born in March following winter rains when forage was highest and before dry conditions arrived, which presumably increased survival (Rubin and others 2000). Survival was lower in lambs born after the peak period (Rubin and others 2000). Another study in New Mexico noted prolonged and irregular breeding timing with lambs born from December to September, suggesting this strategy could be in response to unpredictable rainfall patterns (Lenarz 1979). Timing of births has been related to survival of lambs in some studies. Availability of forage in the spring is important for lamb survival. Changes in precipitation patterns are likely to alter the arrival of peak forage conditions.	1
3. Mismatch potential	What is the separation in time or space between cues that initiate activities related to survival or fecundity and discrete events that provide critical resources?	Available forage does not occur far in advance or at distant locations from breeding.	0
4. Resilience to timing mismatches during breeding	Is reproduction in this species more likely to co-occur with important events?	Adults can breed every year, but a study in Arizona found that there were often no lambs produced the year after a successful breeding so, effectively, breeding occurs less than once a year (Krausman and others 1989).	1

Biotic Interactions: Desert bighorn sheep (*Ovis canadensis mexicana*)

Trait/Quality	Question	Background Info & Explanation of Score	Points
1. Food resources	Are important food resources for this species expected to change?	Desert bighorn sheep eat a wide variety of plant species and vary use with availability. Shrub species are dominant in the diet followed by forbs and then grasses (Krausman and others 1989; Miller and Gaud 1989). They also eat barrel cactus and obtain water from it during hot periods (Warrick and Krausman 1989). Shrubs may be reduced by fire, but forbs and grasses may be encouraged. Shrubs and shrub foliage may also be reduced periodically by drought. Cacti are an important component of forage during drought periods and are resistant to drought.	0

Biotic Interactions: Desert bighorn sheep (*Ovis canadensis mexicana*)			
Trait/Quality	**Question**	**Background Info & Explanation of Score**	**Points**
2. Predators	Are important predator populations expected to change?	Mountain lions are often considered a significant predator (Hayes and others 2000). Coyotes are common predators of lambs. Other predators include bobcats and gray fox. In the Southwest, predation is thought to be primarily opportunistic and not a serious threat (Smith and Krausman 1988). Various predators, which are probably also limited by drought. No expected increases.	0
3. Symbionts	Are populations of symbiotic species expected to change?	No symbionts.	0
4. Disease	Is prevalence of diseases known to cause widespread mortality or reproductive failure in this species expected to change?	Bighorn sheep are prone to transmission of disease from domestic sheep. Many documented cases of high mortality and disease in bighorns, including pneumonia *Pasteurella* sp. (Callan and others 1991), bluetongue (Robinson and others 1967), botulism (Swift and others 2000), chronic sinusitis (Bunch and Allen 1981), and scabies (Lange 1980). Sources of transmission include other ungulates, mites, bot flies, and contaminated water sources. Susceptible to a wide range of diseases. Livestock grazing is limited and is not likely to be an increasing source of infections. Use of limited water (artificial and natural) may be increased with drier conditions and may also increase disease transmission.	1
5. Competitors	Are populations of important competing species expected to change?	Some competition with native ungulates has been documented for food and water, but appears to not be detrimental in the Southwest (Smith and Krausman 1988). Examination of diet in mule deer and bighorns found little overlap (Krausman and others 1989), but there are concerns about competition for water with this species. Conversely, negative competitive effects of domestic livestock have been documented and implicated in bighorn sheep declines (Smith and Krausman 1988). No livestock grazing on BMGR. Bighorn sheep may also compete with other wildlife for water, but extent is unknown and probably limited.	0

Literature Cited

Andrew, N. G., V. C. Bleich, and P. V. August. 1999. Habitat selection by mountain sheep in the Sonoran Desert: implications for conservation in the United States and Mexico. California Wildlife Conservation Bulletin 12:1-30.

Arizona Game and Fish Department. 2006. DRAFT. Arizona's Comprehensive Wildlife Conservation Strategy: 2005-2015. Arizona Game and Fish Department, Phoenix, AZ.

Bagne, K. E., M. M. Friggens, and D. M. Finch. 2011. A system for assessing vulnerability of species (SAVS) to climate change. USDA Forest Service, Rocky Mountain Research Station, Gen. Tech. Rep. RMRS-GTR-257.

Barcikowski, W. and P. S. Nobel. 1984. Water relations of cacti during desiccation: distribution of water in tissues. Botanical Gazette 145:110-115.

Barry M. Goldwater Range (BMGR). 2003. Proposed integrated natural resources management plan: draft EIS. Departments of the Air Force, Navy, and Interior, AZ.

Broyles, B. 1995. Desert wildlife water developments: questioning use in the Southwest. Wildlife Society Bulletin 23:663-675.

Broyes, B. and T. Cutler. 1999. Effect of surface water on desert bighorn sheep in the Cabeza Prieta National Wildlife Refuge, southwestern Arizona. Wildlife Society Bulletin 27:1082-1088.

Bunch, T. D. and S. D. Allen. 1981. Survey of chronic sinusitis-induced skull anomalies in desert bighorn sheep. Journal of the American Veterinary Medicine Association 179:1150-1152.

Cain, J. W., III, P. R. Krausman, J. R. Morgart, B. D. Jansen, and M. P. Pepper. 2008. Responses of desert bighorn sheep to removal of water sources. Wildlife Monographs 171:1-32.

Callan, R. J., T. D. Bunch, G. W. Workman, and R. E. Mock. 1991. Development of pneumonia in desert bighorn sheep after exposure to a flock of exotic wild and domestic sheep. Journal of the American Veterinary Medicine Association 198:1052-1056.

Dewey, T. and L. Ballenger. 1999. "*Ovis canadensis*" [Online]. Animal Diversity Web. Online at: http://animaldiversity.ummz.umich.edu. (Accessed November 18, 2009)

Epps, C. W., D. R. McCullouch, J. D. Wehausen, V. C. Bleich, and J. L. Rechel. 2004. Effects of climate change on population persistence of desert-dwelling mountain sheep in California. Conservation Biology 18:102-113.

Esser, G. 1992. Implications of climate change for production and decomposition in grasslands and coniferous forests. Ecological Applications 2:47-54.

Garfin, G. and M. Lenart. 2007. Climate change effects on Southwest water resources. Southwest Hydrology 6:16-17.

Hansen, M. C. 1982. Desert bighorn sheep: another view. Wildlife Society Bulletin 10:133-140.

Hayes, C. L., E. S. Rubin, M. C. Jorgensen, R. A. Botta, and W. M. Boyce. 2000. Mountain lion predation of bighorn sheep in the Peninsular Ranges, California. The Journal of Wildlife Management 64:954-959.

Hoffmeister, D. F. 1986. Mammals of Arizona. University of Arizona Press and Arizona Game and Fish Dept. 602 p.

Krausman, P. R. and B. D. Leopold. 1986. Habitat components for desert bighorn sheep in the Harquahala Mountains, Arizona. The Journal of Wildlife Management 50:504-508.

Krausman, P. R., B. D. Leopold, R. F. Seegmiller, and S. G. Torres 1989. Relationships between desert bighorn sheep and habitat in western Arizona. Wildlife Monographs 102:3-66.

Lange, R. E., A. V. Sandoval, and W. P. Meleny. 1980. Psoroptic scabies in bighorn sheep (*Ovis canadensis mexicana*) in New Mexico. Journal of Wildlife Disease 16:77-82.

Lenarz, M. S. 1979. Social structure and reproductive strategy in desert bighorn sheep (*Ovis canadensis mexicana*). Journal of Mammalogy 60:671-678.

Liverman, D. M. and K. L. O'Brien. 1991. Global warming and climate change in Mexico. Pages 351-364 In Global Environmental Change. Butterworth-Heinemann Ltd.

McKinney, T., T. W. Smith, and J. D. Hanna. 2001. Precipitation and desert bighorn sheep in the Mazatzal Mountains, Arizona. The Southwestern Naturalist 46:345-353.

McKinney, T., S. R. Boe and J. C. deVos, Jr. 2003. GIS-based evaluation of escape terrain and desert bighorn sheep populations in Arizona. Wildlife Society Bulletin 31:1229-1236.

McLaughlin, S. E. and J. P. Bowers. 1982. Effects of wildfire on a Sonoran Desert plant community. Ecology 63:246-248.

McPherson, G. R. and J. F. Weltzin. 2000. Disturbance and climate change in United States/Mexico borderland plant communities: a state-of-the-knowledge review. USDA Forest Service, Rocky Mountain Research Station, Gen. Tech. Rep. RMRS-GTR-50.

Miller, G. D. and W. S. Gaud. 1989. Composition and variability of desert bighorn sheep diets. Journal of Wildlife Management 53:597-606.

Mitchell, D. L., D. Ivanova, R. Rabin, K. Redmond, and T. J. Brown. 2002. Gulf of California sea surface temperatures and the North American monsoon: mechanistic implications from observations. Journal of Climate 15:2261-2281.

Pinkava, D. J. 1999. Cactaceae cactus family, part three, Cylindropuntia. Journal of the Arizona-Nevada Academy of Science 32:32-47.

O'Brien, C., S. Rosenstock, J. Hervert, J. Bright, and S. Boe. 2005. Landscape-level models of potential habitat for Sonoran pronghorn. Wildlife Society Bulletin 33:24-34.

Robinson, R. M., T. L. Hailey, C. W. Livingston, and J. W. Thomas. 1967. Bluetongue in the desert bighorn sheep. The Journal of Wildlife Management 31:165-168.

Rubin, E. S., W. M. Boyce, and V. C. Bleich. 2000. Reproductive strategies of desert bighorn sheep. Journal of Mammalogy 81:769-786.

Seager, R., T. Ming, I. Held, [and others]. 2007. Model projections of an imminent transition to a more arid climate in southwestern North America. Science 316:1181-1184.

Smith, N. S. and P. R. Krausman. 1988. Desert bighorn sheep: a guide to selected management practices. U.S. Fish and Wildlife Service Biological Report 88.

Smith, S. D., B. Didden-Zopfy, and P. S. Nobel. 1984. High-temperature responses of North American cacti. Ecology 65:643-651.

SWIFT, P. K., J. D. Wehausen, H. B. Ernest, R. S. Singer, A. M. Pauli, H. Kinde, T. E. Rocke, and V. C. Bleich. 2000. Desert bighorn sheep mortality due to presumptive type C botulism in California. Journal of Wildlife Diseases 36:184-189.

Van Devender, T. R. and M. A. Dimmitt. 2006. Final report on conservation of Arizona upland Sonoran Desert habitat: status and threats of buffelgrass (*Pennisetum ciliare*) in Arizona and Sonora. Arizona-Sonora Desert Museum, Tucson, AZ.

Weiss, J. L. and J. T. Overpeck. 2005. Is the Sonoran Desert losing its cool? Global Change Biology 11:2065-2077.

Warrick, G. D. and P. R. Krausman. 1989. Barrel cacti consumption by desert bighorn sheep. Southwestern Naturalist 34:483-486.

Williams, D. G. and Z. Baruch. 2000. African grass invasion in the Americas: ecosystem consequences and the role of ecophysiology. Biological Invasions 2:213-140.

Sonoran Pronghorn
(*Antilocapra americana sonoriensis*)

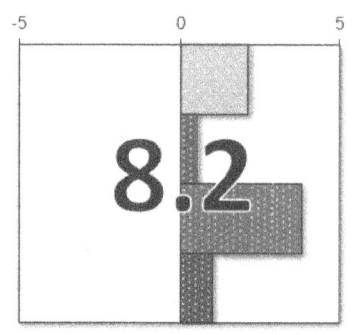

SUMMARY

Vulnerability to drought mortality is a key issue for the Sonoran pronghorn, and associated risk will likely increase in the future. Impacts related to changes in phenology created high vulnerability to population declines with climate change. Natural resilience to droughts and fluctuations in resources is likely incurred by the pronghorn's wide ranging habits, but movements of current populations are restricted by roads and fences. Effects of increased temperatures and more variable rainfall patterns will likely have detrimental effects on populations through changes in forage quantity and quality and increases in direct mortality, particularly to fawns. Improving this species' ability to survive drought conditions will likely be critical to sustaining populations and will require a broad landscape view for management planning as vegetation changes and shifts, although uncertain, occur on a large scale.

VULNERABILITY	Score	Uncertainty
Habitat	**2.1**	14%
Physiology	**1.7**	33%
Phenology	**2.5**	25%
Interactions	**2.0**	40%
Overall	**8.2**	27%

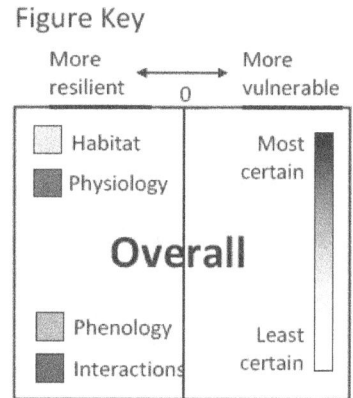

Introduction
Pronghorns are the only members of their family, Antilocapridae. The subspecies, Sonoran pronghorn, was designated as Federally endangered in 1967. There is a semi-captive breeding population, and breeding stock has been translocated from Mexican populations (USFWS 2003). Population surveys conducted from 1992 to 2000 showed a continuing declining trend (USFWS 2003). A population low of 20 animals was estimated for 2002 and was blamed on low forage levels related to drought conditions. Sixty-eight Sonoran pronghorns was the estimated U.S. population for December 2008 (Sonoran Pronghorn Monthly Update, 20 January 2009). A five-year review of the status of the subspecies was initiated by the USFWS in 2008, but results were not available at the time of this report.

Three subpopulations of the subspecies exist, with one in the United States and the other two in Mexico where the species is also designated as endangered (USFWS 2003). Pronghorns mostly occur on the western half of BMGR (2003), but also extend into the west end of the eastern half of the Range as well. They also occur in the bordering Cabeza Prieta National Wildlife Refuge, Organ Pipe Cactus National Monument, and nearby Bureau of Land Management lands. Suitable pronghorn habitat is also available east of Highway 85 on BMGR-East but is not currently utilized (O'Brien and others 2005).

USDA Forest Service RMRS-GTR-284. 2012.

BMGR-East Climate and Projections

- Annual increase in temperature 2.2 °C (4 °F) by 2050 (www.climatewizard.org, A2 emissions, ensembled GCM) and greater evaporation
- No change in average rainfall by 2050 (www.climatewizard.org, A2 emissions, ensembled GCM)
- Sonoran Desert expands northward and eastward, and contracts in the southeast (Weiss and Overpeck 2005)
- More droughts and intense storms (Seager and others 2007)
- Earlier and more intense flooding (Garfin and Lenart 2007; Seager and others 2007)
- Summer monsoon changes unknown (Mitchell and others 2002)
- Grasses favored over shrubs (Esser 1992)
- Increases in invasive grasses and fires (Esser 1992; Williams and Baruch 2000)
- Warmer temperatures and decreased soil moisture in Mexico (Liverman and O'Brien 1991)
- CAM plants (succulents and cacti) will be resilient to increasing temperatures (Smith and others 1984)

A detailed review of projections is in the "Projections of Climate, Disturbance, and Biotic Communities" section of the main document.

Other Threats and Interactions with Climate

Numerous impacts have been proposed to have caused the low population size and continued declines in Sonoran pronghorn. Current populations are so small that any effect detrimental to survival or reproduction is critical to extinction vulnerability. USFWS (1998, 2003) suggested that important impacts include predation, forage availability, barriers to movement, and disease. Other known impacts include disturbance related to illegal border activity and military operations and competition with cattle. A recent study, however, found that pronghorn were mostly habituated to military overflights (Krausman and others 2004). Inbreeding and Allee effects are also potential threats in small populations.

Climate change will likely affect forage availability and quality, which have already been identified as influencing population fluctuations. Increasing variability in rainfall will cause parallel variability in forage, which could be especially damaging to these small populations in drought years. Fires also occur more frequently with increasing rainfall variability and increasing temperatures. Fires probably only reduce forage in the short term and generally increase vegetative growth in post-fire habitats. Interacting effects of fire with grass species, particularly those that are introduced, along with warmer temperatures will enhance grass forage, but grasses are generally not a large component of the diet (Buechner 1950). Increasing fires will threaten other essential habitat elements, including trees for thermal protection and chain-fruit cholla (*Cylindropuntia fulgida*) (and other succulents).

Research Needs

Impacts, both positive and negative, of wildlife waters are not well understood. Effectiveness of artificial waters and forage enhancement plots in mitigating detrimental impacts of drought on Sonoran pronghorn would be particularly applicable with future climate change. Risk of disease transmission at artificial waters needs to be explored. Because migration is speculated to improve the pronghorn's ability to cope with changing conditions, an evaluation of the spatial and temporal variation in forage, interactions with climate, and current land use could provide important information on potential migration corridor enhancements. An assessment of habitat quality under drought conditions would also be helpful. Research on variables that affect predation rates and methods to reduce predation of captive-reared young could provide information for improving survival rates.

Management Implications

Although no recovery criteria or critical habitats have been established, recovery efforts suggested by the USFWS (2003) include: establish forage enhancement plots on BMGR, evaluate reliance on sources of free water, remove coyotes when and where pronghorns are most vulnerable, investigate transplant locations, increase aerial monitoring in Mexico, investigate disease vectors, reduce disturbance during critical periods, and reduce movement barriers. This climate change assessment identifies forage availability, water sources, disease vectors, and movement barriers as the most critical research needs.

BMGR is closed to cattle grazing, which has minimized issues related to grazing competition and disease transmission. Some trespass grazing and grazing by feral burros occurs (BMGR 2003), but is unlikely to have significant or altered impacts unless there is increased contact that results in disease transmission such as through attraction to a localized water source.

Management often restricts activities during periods when disturbance can have the greatest negative impacts, such as during breeding. The adjacent Cabeza Prieta National Wildlife Refuge institutes fawning season closures on March 15 to July 15. Changes in climate, however, are likely to alter breeding timing, particularly earlier, so closure dates should be reevaluated.

Although not currently a major threat at BMGR, fire and its interaction with introduced plants can significantly alter vegetation and may be an emerging issue that warrants monitoring. At least in the short term, fire promotes grasses over shrubs, shrubs being the preferred forage of Sonoran pronghorn. In addition, succulents, which are an important water source, are prone to fire mortality and often require shrubs as nursery plants for establishment, thus increasing recovery time following fires. Both of these resources are limited and may be important to pronghorn survival during drought periods. BMGR already has programs to control some invasive plants, and these efforts will be essential to protecting native habitats. Roadsides are likely locations where invasives can spread as they serve as corridors to seed transfer and provide water through run-off. Fire-prone invasive species should be included in control, and increased fire risk should be evaluated for critical pronghorn habitats such as those dominated by palo verde and cacti.

Drought conditions, which are expected to increase, are limiting, thus management actions to mitigate drought conditions, such as water management, providing migration corridors, or forage enhancements, will be critical. Forage enhancement plots and wildlife waters are part of current management and should be evaluated for their ability to mitigate negative impacts of severe drought. Additional management should focus on desert trees, as these provide shade important for pronghorn survival during hot conditions. Although direct effects such as heat and disease may have negative impacts, changes in the quantity and quality of vegetation for forage will likely be the most important climate change impact on pronghorn populations. Shrubs and succulents are particularly valuable for survival. Projections for vegetation, however, are dependent on the interactions of complex factors such as fire and invasive grasses on current conditions, as well as on changes to seasonal precipitation, which are still difficult to predict with current climate models. Although it is unknown how vegetation will ultimately respond, it is likely that over a large area, there will be both beneficial and detrimental vegetation shifts for pronghorns. Management of populations therefore may best anticipate uncertain future changes by planning over a broad area, including lands adjacent to BMGR and particularly areas where droughts will have lower impact. These include areas that are currently inaccessible to pronghorn, thus enhancement of migration opportunities is essential to drought resilience.

Habitat: Sonoran pronghorn (*Antilocapra americana sonoriensis*)			
Trait/Quality	**Question**	**Background Info & Explanation of Score**	**Points**
1. Area and distribution: *breeding*	Is the area or location of the associated vegetation type used for breeding activities by this species expected to change?	In southwestern Arizona, Sonoran pronghorn are associated with vegetation such as big galleta grass, creosote bush, bursage, and saltbush. Pronghorns occupy similar habitat in Sonora, Mexico, where they are associated with stable sand dunes interspersed with grasslands (Hoffmeister 1986). They also occur in creosotebush-bursage habitat year-round and utilize areas containing palo verde-mixed cacti plant associations in spring and summer (Federal Register, 7 September 1994, p. 46266). Sonoran desert habitats are expected to expand northward in the United States. Expansion areas will not be available to pronghorns because of roads and fences.	0
2. Area and distribution: *non-breeding*	Is the area or location of the associated vegetation type used for non-breeding activities by this species expected to change?	Same as above.	0
3. Habitat components: *breeding*	Are specific habitat components required for breeding expected to change within associated vegetation type?	Dense shrubs are important fawning locations for *Antilocarpa amercana* in sagebrush habitats (Alldredge 1994), but relationship is unknown for Sonoran populations. Open habitats may also be associated with increased survival of adults as predators are more easily detected and avoided. Palo verde is drought deciduous. Dry conditions and fires may reduce shrubs or shrub cover with mixed results for breeding success. Likely depends on distribution of shrub clumps, but distribution of shrub patches is difficult to project.	0
4. Habitat components: *non-breeding*	Are other specific habitat components required for survival during non-breeding periods expected to change within associated vegetation type?	Washes and habitats with palo verde and chain fruit cholla are preferred and home range size is reduced compared to other habitats indicating greater habitat quality (Hervert and others 2005). Availability of free water reportedly is a critical factor (Hoffmeister 1986) and pronghorns are known to drink from artificial water sources (Morgart and others 2005), but water requirements are not well known. Requirement of free-standing water is assumed for at least some periods, and availability of this water is likely to decrease.	1
5. Habitat quality	Within habitats occupied, are features of the habitat associated with better reproductive success or survival expected to change?	Succulence of forage has been suggested as a measure of habitat quality that incurs greater reproductive success (Kitchen 1974), and has also been related to frequency of drinking (Beale and Smith 1970). Drier conditions and reduction in natural waters are projected. Trees provide shade for survival in hot weather. Fires fueled by invasive grasses are likely to be detrimental to shrubs and trees, although extent of this increased fire risk at BMGR is unknown. In addition, starting in April, pronghorns need to drink water because they switch from forbs to shrub forage.	1

Habitat: Sonoran pronghorn (*Antilocapra americana sonoriensis*)			
Trait/Quality	**Question**	**Background Info & Explanation of Score**	**Points**
6. Ability to colonize new areas	What is the potential for this species to disperse?	Historically, pronghorn likely moved to wetter regions with more succulent forage, such as along permanent rivers, before movements were limited by fences and highways (USFWS 2003). Pronghorns have a high capacity to disperse, but there are already many barriers to dispersal. Barriers are unlikely to be reduced with changes in climate and may even be increased with related increases in border activities and increasing human populations. Overall, limited ability to colonize new areas.	1
7. Migratory or transitional habitats	Does this species require additional habitats during migration that are separated from breeding and non-breeding habitats?	No transitional habitats known.	0

Physiology: Sonoran pronghorn (*Antilocapra americana sonoriensis*)			
Trait/Quality	**Question**	**Background Info & Explanation of Score**	**Points**
1. Physiological thresholds	Are limiting physiological conditions expected to change?	Generally adapted to hot and dry desert conditions. Drought has been implicated in mortality due directly to heat stress or indirectly to reduced forage (Bright and Hervert 2005). Young may also be prone to heat-related mortality above 40 °C (Wilson and Krausman 2008). Hotter temperatures and more frequent droughts are predicted.	1
2. Sex ratio	Is sex ratio determined by temperature?	No.	0
3. Exposure to weather-related disturbance	Are disturbance events (e.g., severe storms, fires, floods) that affect survival or reproduction expected to change?	No known effects of disturbance events.	0
4. Limitations to daily activity period	Are projected temperature or precipitation regimes that influence activity period of species expected to change?	Alternating periods of feeding and rest occur throughout the day, with fairly continuous feeding in the early morning and late afternoon, and longer rest periods at night (Davis 1974). They have both nocturnal and diurnal activities with peaks at dawn and dusk, particularly during hot periods (Buechner 1950; Kitchen 1974). Reduce activities during hot parts of the day in summer and winter, compensating with a switch to more activity during crepuscular periods (Wilson 2009). This flexibility in behavior may limit reductions in activity periods associated with climate, although relationship is not well known.	0

Physiology: Sonoran pronghorn (*Antilocapra americana sonoriensis*)			
Trait/Quality	**Question**	**Background Info & Explanation of Score**	**Points**
5. Survival during resource fluctuation	Does this species have flexible strategies to cope with variation in resources across multiple years?	Probably initiate migration to other areas to cope with changing resources, but migratory behavior is now considerably limited by fences and roads.	1
6. Metabolic rates	What is this species metabolic rate?	Moderate endothermic.	0

Phenology: Sonoran pronghorn (*Antilocapra americana sonoriensis*)			
Trait/Quality	**Question**	**Background Info & Explanation of Score**	**Points**
1. Cues	Does this species use temperature or moisture cues to initiate activities related to fecundity or survival (e.g., hibernation, migration, breeding)?	Not known what triggers breeding. Earlier timing in Sonoran populations is a significant difference from northern populations. Although breeding timing may be sensitive to temperature or moisture, they may not be direct cues.	0
2. Breeding timing	Are activities related to species' fecundity or survival tied to discrete resource peaks (e.g., food, breeding sites) that are expected to change?	Rainfall events are likely important in fawn survival, so it is likely that timing of breeding to these events is important. In addition, starting in April, pronghorns need to drink water, because they switch from forbs to shrub forage (Wilson 2009). Rainfall quantity and timing is likely to become more variable.	1
3. Mismatch potential	What is the separation in time or space between cues that initiate activities related to survival or fecundity and discrete events that provide critical resources?	Breeding is separated in time from fawning to some extent. Fawn survival is dependent on predator levels and mortality has been linked to drought; thus, successful timing may relate to precipitation and/or predator populations, which cannot be adjusted for. No strong probability of mismatch, but no particular traits to reduce mismatch in timing either.	0
4. Resilience to timing mismatches during breeding	Is reproduction in this species more likely to co-occur with important events?	One breeding event per year or less.	1

Biotic Interactions: Sonoran pronghorn (*Antilocapra americana sonoriensis*)			
Trait/Quality	**Question**	**Background Info & Explanation of Score**	**Points**
1. Food resources	Are important food resources for this species expected to change?	Sonoran pronghorns eat a variety of desert plants, including cacti, pigweed (*Amaranthus palmeri*), ragweed (*Ambrosia* sp.), locoweed (*Astragalus* sp.), brome (*Bromus* sp.), and snakeweed (*Gutierrezia sarothrae*) (USFWS 1998). Grass is only a minor component of the pronghorn diet (Buechner 1950). In addition, Sonoran pronghorns are known to switch preferred forage species with variations in climate (deVos and Miller 2005; Hervert and others 2005). Cacti, and in particular chain fruit cholla (*Cylindropuntia fulgida*), provide a source of water (Pinkava 1999) and are important during hot and dry conditions (Hervert and others 1997). During droughts, cacti are a major component of the diet (Hughes and Smith 1990). Greater variability in rainfall will increase forage availability in some years, but drought periods will reduce forage. Fires may increase cover of grass, but grass is only a minor forage component. Cacti are an important component of forage during drought periods and are resistant to drought although water content will be reduced. Overall reductions predicted.	1
2. Predators	Are important predator populations expected to change?	In American pronghorn (*A. a. americana*), coyotes did not depredate adults, but could successfully kill fawns up to 45 days old (Byers 1997). Young pronghorn raised from captivity and released, however, seem to be vulnerable and are often killed by coyotes. There is evidence of predation by coyotes, bobcats, and mountain lions. Coyote populations are likely somewhat resilient to changes in climate given their wide range of tolerances and prey species. Predation rates are high and may not be expected to increase significantly.	0
3. Symbionts	Are populations of symbiotic species expected to change?	No symbionts.	0
4. Disease	Is prevalence of diseases known to cause widespread mortality or reproductive failure in this species expected to change?	Testing of individuals revealed presence of bluetongue and epizootic hemorrhagic disease, which are both potentially fatal (USFWS 2003). Biting midges (*Culicoides* spp.) are suspected as the vector for these diseases and breed in wet areas. Bluetongue is also transmitted to pronghorn from cattle (USFWS 1998). Increasing reliance of water sources where biting midges (vectors) breed and increased attraction to those areas due to water limitations may increase bluetongue infection rates.	1
5. Competitors	Are populations of important competing species expected to change?	Competition is strong with domestic sheep and weaker with cattle (Buechner 1950). Cattle eat some forbs and other browse species that are preferred by pronghorns, but pronghorns seem to represent little competition as grasses preferred by cattle comprise only a small proportion of their diet (Buechner 1950). Although pronghorn have been observed to be able to sustain populations on overgrazed cattle lands (Buechner 1950), cattle may present more of a competitive problem (Yoakum 2004). Cattle and domestic sheep are usually not present on BMGR. Interactions with other ungulates are likely limited.	0

Literature Cited

Alldredge, A. W., R. D. Deblinger, and J. Peterson. 1991. Birth and fawn bed site selection by pronghorns in a sagebrush-steppe community. Journal of Wildlife Management 55:222-227.

Bagne, K. E., M. M. Friggens, and D. M. Finch. 2011. A system for assessing vulnerability of species (SAVS) to climate change. USDA Forest Service, Rocky Mountain Research Station, Gen. Tech. Rep. RMRS-GTR-257.

Barry M. Goldwater Range (BMGR). 2003. Proposed integrated natural resources management plan: draft EIS. Departments of the Air Force, Navy, and Interior, Arizona.

Beale, D. and A. Smith. 1970. Forage use, water consumption, and productivity of pronghorn antelope in western Utah. Journal of Wildlife Management 34:570-582.

Bowers, J. E. and R. M. Turner. 2001. Dieback and episodic mortality of *Cercidium microphyllum* (foothill paloverde), a dominant Sonoran Desert tree. Journal of the Torrey Botanical Society 128:128-140.

Bright, J. L. and J. J. Hervert. 2005. Adult and fawn mortality of Sonoran pronghorn. Wildlife Society Bulletin 33(1):43-50.

Buechner, H. K. 1950. Life history, ecology, and range use of the pronghorn antelope in Trans-Pecos Texas. American Midland Naturalist 43:257-354.

deVos, J. C. and W. H. Miller. 2005. Habitat use and survival of Sonoran pronghorn in years with above-average rainfall. Wildlife Society Bulletin 33:35-42.

Esser, G. 1992. Implications of climate change for production and decomposition in grasslands and coniferous forests. Ecological Applications 2:47-54.

Fox, L. M., P. R. Krausman, M. L. Morrison, and R. M. Kattnig. 2000. Water and nutrient content of forage in Sonoran pronghorn habitat, Arizona. California Fish and Game 86(4):216-232.

Garfin, G. and M. Lenart. 2007. Climate change effects on Southwest water resources. Southwest Hydrology 6:16-17.

Hervert, J. J., J. L. Bright, R. S. Henry, L. A. Piest, and M. T. Brown. 2005. Home-range and habitat-use patterns of Sonoran pronghorn in Arizona. Wildlife Society Bulletin 33:8-15.

Hoffmeister, D. F. 1986. Mammals of Arizona. University of Arizona Press and Arizona Game and Fish Dept. 602 p.

Hughes, K. S. and N. S. Smith. 1990. Sonoran pronghorn use of habitat in Southwest Arizona. Report to Cabeza Prieta National Wildlife Refuge, Ajo, AZ.

Kitchen, D. W. 1974. Social behavior and ecology of the pronghorn. Wildlife Monographs 38:3-96.

Krausman, P. R., L. K. Harris, C. L. Blasch, K. K. G. Koenen, and J. Francine. 2004. Effects of military operations on behavior and hearing of endangered Sonoran pronghorn. Wildlife Monographs 157:1-41.

Liverman, D. M. and K. L. O'Brien. 1991. Global warming and climate change in Mexico. Pages 351-364 in Global Environmental Change. Butterworth-Heinemann Ltd.

McLaughlin, S. E. and J. P. Bowers. 1982. Effects of wildfire on a Sonoran Desert plant community. Ecology 63:246-248.

McPherson, G. R. and J. F. Weltzin. 2000. Disturbance and climate change in United States/Mexico borderland plant communities: a state-of-the-knowledge review. USDA Forest Service, Rocky Mountain Research Station, Gen. Tech. Rep. RMRS-GTR-50.

Mitchell, D. L., D. Ivanova, R. Rabin, K. Redmond, and T. J. Brown. 2002. Gulf of California sea surface temperatures and the North American monsoon: mechanistic implications from observations. Journal of Climate 15:2261-2281.

Morgart, J. R., J. J. Hervert, P. R. Krausman, J. L. Bright, and R. S. Henry. 2005. Sonoran pronghorn use of anthropogenic and natural waters. Wildlife Society Bulletin 33:51-60.

Pinkava, D. J. 1999. Cactaceae cactus family, part three, Cylindropuntia. Journal of the Arizona-Nevada Academy of Science 32(1):32-47.

O'Brien, C., S. Rosenstock, J. Hervert, J. Bright, and S. Boe. 2005. Landscape-level models of potential habitat for Sonoran pronghorn. Wildlife Society Bulletin 33:24-34.

Seager, R., T. Ming, I. Held, [and others]. 2007. Model projections of an imminent transition to a more arid climate in southwestern North America. Science 316:1181-1184.

Swetnam, T. W. and J. L Betancourt. 1990. Fire-southern oscillation relations in the southwestern United States. Science 249:1017-1020.

U.S. Fish and Wildlife Service (USFWS). 1998. Recovery criteria and estimates of time for recovery actions for the Sonoran pronghorn. U.S. Fish and Wildlife Service, Region 2, Albuquerque, NM.

U.S. Fish and Wildlife Service (USFWS). 2003. Supplement and amendment to the 1998 final revised Sonoran pronghorn recovery plan (*Antilocapra americana sonoriensis*). U.S. Fish and Wildlife Service, Albuquerque, NM.

Weiss, J. L. and J. T. Overpeck. 2005. Is the Sonoran Desert losing its cool? Global Change Biology 11:2065-2077.

Williams, D. G. and Z. Baruch. 2000. African grass invasion in the Americas: ecosystem consequences and the role of ecophysiology. Biological Invasions 2:213-140.

Wilson, R. R. and P. R. Krausman. 2008. Possibility of heat-related mortality in desert ungulates. Journal of the Arizona-Nevada Academy of Science 40:12-15.

Wilson, R. R., P. R. Krausman, and J. R. Morgart. 2009. Behavior and activity budgets of Sonoran pronghorns (*Antilocapra americana sonoriensis*). Southwestern Naturalist 54:45-54.

Yoakum, J. 2004. Management plans, environmental impact statements and guides. Pages 541-569 In B. W. O'Gara and J. D. Yoakum, eds., Pronghorn Ecology and Management. University Press of Colorado, Boulder.

Acuña Cactus
(*Echinomastus erectrocentrus var. acunensis*)

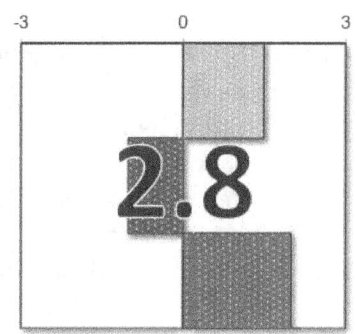

SUMMARY

Acuña cactus is vulnerable to declines associated with future climate change. Although well adapted to hot temperatures and limited water, increasing fires and possible declines in animal dispersers and pollinators are likely to be detrimental. Management that addresses fire risk and improves conditions for recruitment will be important for sustaining populations.

VULNERABILITY	Score	Uncertaint
Habitat	**1.5**	25%
Physiology	**-1.0**	33%
Interactions	**2.0**	33%
Overall	**2.8**	**30%**

Figure Key

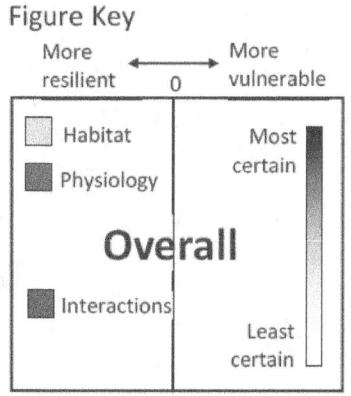

Introduction

Acuña cactus is a candidate for listing as a Federally endangered or threatened species and may occur on BMGR. It is restricted to knolls and gravel ridges between major washes in Sonoran desertscrub habitat. Nearby populations are reported from the Sand Tank and Sauceda Mountains on lands administered by the Bureau of Land Management, as well as Organ Pipe Cactus National Monument (CBD 2002).

BMGR-East Climate Projections Used for Assessment

- Annual increase in temperature 2.2 °C (4 °F) by 2050 (www.climatewizard.org, A2 emissions, ensembled GCM) and greater evaporation
- No change in average rainfall by 2050 (www.climatewizard.org, A2 emissions, ensembled GCM)
- Sonoran Desert expands northward and eastward, and contracts in the southeast (Weiss and Overpeck 2005)
- More droughts and intense storms (Seager and others 2007)
- Earlier and more intense flooding (Garfin and Lenart 2007; Seager and others 2007)
- Summer monsoon changes unknown (Mitchell and others 2002)
- Grasses favored over shrubs (Esser 1992)
- Increases in invasive grasses and fires (Esser 1992; Williams and Baruch 2000)

A detailed review of projections is in the "Projections of Climate, Disturbance, and Biotic Communities" section of the main text.

Other Threats and Interactions with Climate Change

Threats identified by USFWS are grazing, collection, mining, recreation, and land development (CBD 2002). Acuña cactus populations may be declining at the nearby Organ Pipe Cactus National Monument (CBD 2002). Reasons for decline in this protected population are unclear; perhaps natural limiting factors have been exacerbated by dry conditions. For example, impacts from native grazers and insect borers may increase during dry years. In addition, seed germination can depend on temperature, innate dormancy, light, and ingestion by animals (Rojas-Aréchiga and Vázquez-Yanes 2000). None of these threats is likely a major concern on BMGR except perhaps off-highway vehicle use. Illegal immigrant traffic and associated border patrol activities may similarly threaten populations.

Johnson (1992) found the number of flowers produced annually to be positively correlated with annual rainfall. Water storage or cactus volume was also correlated with flowering, further indicating that flowering is limited by water availability (Johnson 1992). Furthermore, germination may be highest following monsoonal rains (Johnson 1993). Monsoonal rain is important and, although not well projected into the future, it is expected that rainfall timing will shift. There should still be some years with adequate rainfall for recruitment, although conditions for germination and seedling survival are not well known.

One of the largest threats on Federal lands may be the interaction of invasive grass species with fire, a threat also noted in the petition to list the species as endangered (CBD 2002). Invasive grasses such as buffelgrass (*Pennisetum ciliare*) encourage frequent, high intensity fires that convert desert scrub to grasslands and do not allow desert species time to recover. More arid locations may be expected to support a different fire regime. Higher fuel loads associated with the introduced buffelgrass increase fire intensity and may result in much higher initial mortality. More importantly, invasion by these grasses rather than just the occasional high fuel loads that occur following heavy rainfall years can change fire regimes to ones that are not compatible with many desert plants.

Research Needs

Limiting factors are unknown and need to be evaluated, as protected populations seem to be in decline. Conditions favorable to recruitment will be important and can help inform management related to habitat enhancement, restoration, or post-fire rehabilitation. An assessment of fire risk could also identify needs and target areas for management.

Management Implications

Potential for occurrence of acuña cactus on lands managed as part of BMGR should be evaluated. Management related to fire risk will be important, at least in some locations. Fire threat will depend on various factors, including topography, surrounding vegetation, proximity to introduced grasses, and soils. Invasive grasses can also compete for water and should be controlled in the vicinity of cactus populations. Acuña cactus should also be included in post-fire planning. Protection of multiple populations will be important for this species as drought and other stresses may result in local population extinctions.

Habitat: Acuña cactus (*Echinomastus erectrocentrus* var. *acunensis*)			
Trait/Quality	Question	Background Info & Explanation of Score	Points
1. Increased droughts and warming.	Is this species associated with wetlands, riparian areas, or other mesic environments expected to decline?	No. Acuña cactus occur on well-drained granite substrates on knolls at elevations ranging from 397-610 m (1300-2000 ft) (CBD 2002).	0
2. Habitat elements	Does this species require specialized microsites?	Isolated by occurrence on specialized soil types (CBD 2002).	1
3 Ability to colonize new areas	What is this species dispersal ability?	Cactus seeds or fruit are transported by animals, including ants (Rojas-Aréchiga and Vázquez-Yanes 2000). Dispersal will depend on climate change effects on these species.	1
4. Seedling conditions	Do seedlings require different conditions from mature individuals (shade, moisture, fires, nurse plants, etc)?	Various conditions that improve microsite moisture have been associated with cactus germination, including nurse plants and rocks (Rojas-Aréchiga and Carlos Vázquez-Yanes 2000). No information found for this species, but rocky habitats may fulfill this function. No expected change.	0

Physiology: Acuña cactus (*Echinomastus erectrocentrus* var. *acunensis*)			
Trait/Quality	Question	Background Info & Explanation of Score	Points
1. Exposure to disturbance	Are disturbance events that result in direct mortality or reproductive failure expected to change?	Although many cacti may live through wildfires in semi-desert grasslands, annual mortality for many species is increased and may be more important than short-term effects (Thomas 2006). Fires are expected to increase.	1
2. Adaptations to survive water limitations	Does this species possess adaptations to increase survival during droughts (i.c., waxy leaves, water storage, cavitation, drought deciduous)?	Yes. Cactus have specialized adaptations for dry conditions.	-1
3. Photosynthetic pathway	Which photosynthetic pathway does this species use?	CAM.	-1

Interactions: Acuña cactus (*Echinomastus erectrocentrus* var. *acunensis*)			
Trait/Quality	**Question**	**Background Info & Explanation of Score**	**Points**
1. Pollination	What is the pollination vector?	Flowers are self-incompatible and insect pollinators are required. Insect pollinators were mostly solitary bees from the family Anthophoridae (Johnson 1992).	1
2. Disease	Any known diseases/parasites that result in mass mortality related to temperature or precipitation?	Not known for this species.	0
3. Competitors	Are populations of important competing species expected to change?	Hedgehog cactus flowering was not found to interfere with pollination of this species (Johnson 1992). May compete for water with grasses. Grasses expected to increase in some areas.	1

Literature Cited

Center for Biological Diversity (CBD). 2002. Petition to list the acuña cactus as endangered. Unpublished report.

Esser, G. 1992. Implications of climate change for production and decomposition in grasslands and coniferous forests. Ecological Applications 2:47-54.

Garfin, G. and M. Lenart. 2007. Climate change effects on Southwest water resources. Southwest Hydrology 6:16-17.

Johnson, R. A. 1992. Pollination and reproductive ecology of acuña cactus, *Echinomastus erectrocentrus* var. *acunensis* (Cactaceae). International Journal of Plant Science 153:400-408.

Johnson, R. A., M. A. Baker, D. J. Pinkava, and G.A. Ruffner. 1993. Seedling establishment, mortality, growth, and flower production in acuña cactus, *Ecinomastus erectrocentrus* var. *acunensis*. Pages 170-180 in R.Sivinski and K. Lightfoot, eds., Proceedings of the Southwestern Rare and Endangered Plant Conference, Santa Fe, NM.

Mitchell, D. L., D. Ivanova, R. Rabin, K. Redmond, and T. J. Brown. 2002. Gulf of California sea surface temperatures and the North American monsoon: mechanistic implications from observations. Journal of Climate 15:2261-2281.

Rojas-Aréchiga, M. and C. Vázquez-Yanes. 2000. Cactus seed germination: a review. Journal of Arid Environments 44:85-104.

Seager, R., T. Mingfang, I. Held, [and others]. 2007. Model projections of an imminent transition to a more arid climate in southwestern North America. Science 316:1181-1184.

Thomas, P. A. 2006. Mortality over 16 years of cacti in a burnt desert grassland. Plant Ecology 183:9-17.

Weiss, J. L. and J. T. Overpeck. 2005. Is the Sonoran Desert losing its cool? Global Change Biology 11:2065-2077.

Williams, D. G. and Z. Baruch. 2000. African grass invasion in the Americas: ecosystem consequences and the role of ecophysiology. Biological Invasions 2:213-140.

www.ingramcontent.com/pod-product-compliance
Lightning Source LLC
Chambersburg PA
CBHW081217280526
45787CB00006B/2427